Table of Contents

CHAPTERS OF REVELATION RELATED TO HISTORY

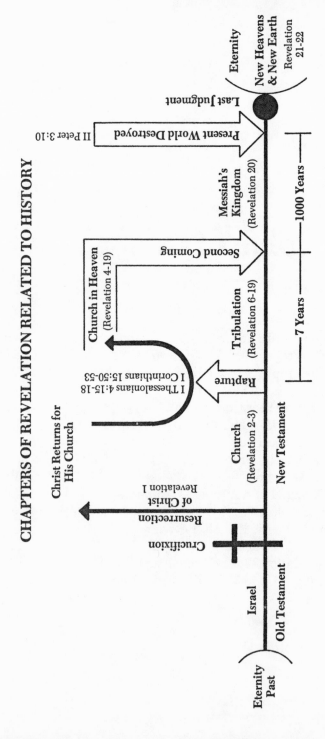

GOD'S OUTLINE OF HISTORY

Eternity Past

Israel
Old Testament

Crucifixion

Resurrection
of Christ
Revelation 1

Christ Returns for
His Church

Church
(Revelation 2-3)
New Testament

Rapture
I Thessalonians 4:15-18
I Corinthians 15:50-53

Church in Heaven
(Revelation 4-19)

Tribulation
(Revelation 6-19)

7 Years

Second Coming

Messiah's
Kingdom
(Revelation 20)

1000 Years

Present World Destroyed
II Peter 3:10

Last Judgment

Eternity
New Heavens
& New Earth
Revelation
21-22

Preface

In this book I have set myself the task of examining Hal Lindsey's method of interpreting the Bible. The opening chapter offers a short sketch of Lindsey's vision of the future as it comes to expression especially in *The Late Great Planet Earth*. The next chapter deals with the proper method of interpreting the Bible. Lindsey claims to interpret Biblical prophecy "literally." Is his approach the proper method, or does Scripture itself point in a different direction?

There are more questions that arise from an evaluation of Hal Lindsey's writings. How are we to read the book of Revelation? What does the Bible say about the future of Israel? Are we to await a millennial kingdom or thousand-year reign of Christ? Answering these questions will at the same time show us how to respond to Lindsey's writings.

On the basis of Scripture, Lindsey's view of the future must be rejected. But it is not enough to shake one's head. This book therefore aims to give guidance; it aims to show how we are to read Lindsey's favorite passages in Daniel, Revelation, Ezekiel, and Zechariah, using Scripture to interpret Scripture.

Through this book, I hope to reach many Christians who wish to bow to the authority of Scripture. "First of all you must understand this, that no prophecy of scripture is a matter of one's own interpretation" (I Pet. 1:20).

May the Lord use this book to further a proper understanding of the riches of His Word!

1

The Future According to Hal Lindsey

In this chapter we will briefly summarize Hal Lindsey's expectations for the future. He has outlined his views and given a systematic interpretation of Revelation in a book entitled *There's a New World Coming*. This book will not be our main concern; a quick overview of its contents will suffice.

Rather, our main concern will be with Lindsey's book entitled *The Late Great Planet Earth*, in which he describes the events that will occur during the last world war, which will precede Christ's final, majestic return. Later in this Chapter we will summarize this book, which does not restrict itself to the prophecies of the apostle John.

God's Historical Plan

Lindsey's view of the development of history is to be found in the diagram (p. 6) reprinted from *There's a New World Coming*. The following remarks will clarify how the Book of Revelation functions as the source of Lindsey's scheme of history.

In Revelation 1:19 we read "Write the things which you have seen, and the things which are, and the things which shall happen after these things." The phrase "the things which are" alludes to the seven churches described in chapters 2 and 3 of Revelation. According to Lindsey, these churches represent the condition of the Church during the various stages of her existence from A.D. 33 to the Tribulation. "The things which shall happen after these things" refers to all the events after Christ takes His believers out of the world, events which will precede Christ's second coming (Rev. 4-19).

Chapters 4 and 5 set the stage for the final judgment of the world. The Church, the main theme of the first three chapters, disappears in chapter 4, to reappear finally in chapter 19. But where is the Church during the ravages of the earth described in chapters 6-19? Lindsey claims, with reference to I Thessalonians 4:15-17 and I Corinthians 15:50-3, that the believers will be taken up to meet Christ in the sky just before the Tribulation. (This event is called the Rapture.) In this first phase of Christ's return, He will come secretly like a thief in the night. It will not be until the second phase, when He returns with majesty and power, that every eye will see Him.

The events occurring immediately after the Rapture are described in chapter 5. Then, when the seven seals of the scroll are broken, the judgments of the last stage of world history are revealed. The period of history that begins in chapter 6 is called the Tribulation, a period of seven years' duration. Its three stages of increasingly severe sentence are represented by the seven seals, the seven trumpets, and the seven bowls.

When the first seal is opened, a white horse appears, whose armed rider is given a crown, whereupon he goes forth to conquer (Rev. 6:2). According to Lindsey, there are two Antichrists. The rider of the white horse is the

Fuehrer, the Antichrist from Europe. This Antichrist, ruling from Rome, will have political and economic control of the world. The other Antichrist will be a Jew posing as a religious prophet.

In chapter 13, both of these Antichrists appear on stage. The first rules over the revived Roman empire, which has developed from the original ten countries of the European Common Market. This ruler receives his power from the dragon, which is worshiped by humanity because it is able, by means of its satanic, superior wisdom, to bring the overwhelming world crisis to an end. But three and a half years later, the sheep's clothing is tossed aside to reveal the ruler's true nature: he is a ruthless tyrant who persecutes the believers.

The second beast represents the Jewish Antichrist. He is a false prophet who imitates Christ. (This is shown by the beast's having the two horns of the Lamb.) He helps to establish the universal worship of the Roman dictator.

The emptying of the seven bowls in Revelation 16 culminates in the Battle of Armageddon, the last great war. The climax of this third world war will be a very severe earthquake, presumably caused by nuclear weapons.

The believers reappear in chapter 19. The marriage supper is eaten by Christ, those saints who have survived the Tribulation (i.e. the Israelites spoken of in Revelation 7, the 144,000, and those who came to faith through them), and the Church which was taken up before the Tribulation began. This supper marks the beginning of the thousand-year reign of God on earth.

The time to judge the unbelievers now arrives. Christ returns to the Mount of Olives to execute the sentences. He begins by throwing both Antichrists into the lake of fire (Rev. 19:20). Satan is judged at the same time.

An angel captures him and binds him for a thousand years. He is unbound and thrown into the lake of fire at the end of the thousand-year reign. The last judgment follows, in which the unbelievers are raised from the dead (the second resurrection) and thrown into the lake of fire.

After describing these judgments, John gives us a glimpse of the holy city, the New Jerusalem, in chapters 21 and 22.

This, then, is a brief summary of Hal Lindsey's book *There's a New World Coming.* We will now turn our attention to his understanding of the course of events at the time of the last great war.

"Israel's Treaty with Hell"

Lindsey traces the events that will lead to the Battle of Armageddon. He makes use of the prophecy of Daniel 9 to do this:

> Some 2500 years ago the prophet Daniel said that a prince would come to power from the people who would destroy the city of Jerusalem and the second Temple (Daniel 9:27). The Romans under Titus did the destroying, so the coming prince would have to be someone out of the Roman culture. This Roman prince . . . will come to power just before the return of Christ. He will make "a strong covenant" with the Israelis, guaranteeing their safety and protection. The word translated "strong covenant" has the idea of a treaty or mutual protection pact. The Israelis will then be permitted to reinstitute the sacrifice and offering aspect of the law of Moses. This demands that the Temple be rebuilt, because according to the law of Moses, sacrifices can be offered only in the Temple at Jerusalem.

Apparently all this will be done under the protection of the Antichrist of Rome (PE, 140-1).

Lindsey states that the Tribulation of seven years' duration will begin at the moment when the Israeli leader and the Roman dictator sign the treaty. The Antichrist will find an ingenious solution to the problem of the Middle East. The whole world will then rally around the dictator because he will have brought peace. Bolstered by this public adoration, the Roman tyrant will go to the temple in Jerusalem, where he will proclaim himself to be the incarnation of God. Lindsey here refers to II Thessalonians 2:4 and Matthew 24:15. This proclamation will be the sign that Armageddon is imminent (PE, 142).

The Phases of the Last War

Lindsey distinguishes five phases in the escalation leading up to the Battle of Armageddon. In Phase I, an Arab-African confederacy attacks Israel. Reference is made to Daniel 11:40: "At the time of the end the king of the south shall attack him [Israeli leader]." Lindsey inserts the phrase in parentheses. The king of the south represents the Egyptian leader of the Arab-African confederacy.

In Phase II Russia will counterattack by sea through the Dardanelles, and by land from the Middle East. Lindsey reads this, too, in Daniel 11:40: "But the king of the north [i.e. Russia] shall rush upon him [the Israeli leader] like a whirlwind, with chariots [mechanized army] and horsemen [cavalry], and with many ships." According to Lindsey, Russia and its allies will use the events as an excuse to launch an invasion of the Middle East.

Reference is also made to Ezekiel 38:10-12, where, according to Lindsey, the prophet describes "the plot of the Russian leaders against revived Israel" (PE, 143). The Russians will be enticed by the material wealth of Israel. Their goal will be, as Ezekiel prophesies, "to seize spoil and carry off plunder" (PE, 143). At the time of the Antichrist's rule, Israel will be one of the richest countries of the world. The potential mineral wealth of Israel is incredible: "The value of the mineral deposits in the Dead Sea alone has been estimated at one trillion, two hundred and seventy billion dollars. This is more than the combined wealth of France, England, and the United States!" (PE, 143, 145).

The Russians will march through the Middle East in a "blitzkrieg" manner. This is evident from Daniel 11:40-1: "And he [Russians] shall come into countries [of the Middle East] and shall overflow and pass through. He shall come into the glorious land [Israel]. And tens of thousands shall fall." The same thing is prophesied in Ezekiel 38:14-16.

In Phase III Russia double-crosses Egypt, the leader of the United Arab Republic. Daniel predicts this action when he says:

> He shall stretch out his hand against the countries [i.e. Arab countries of the Middle East], and the land of Egypt shall not escape. He [Russian leader] shall become ruler of the treasures of gold and silver, and all the precious things of Egypt; and the Libyans [African Arabs] and the Ethiopians [African blacks] shall follow in his train (Daniel 11:42-3).

Phase IV is preceded by the beginning of the conquest of Africa via a Russian attack to the West and to the South. The Russian commander will receive alarming news while the greater part of his army is in Egypt, according to Daniel 11:44. He hears tidings out of the "East" (the Orient mobilizing) and out of the "North" (the Roman confederacy mobilizing) and regroups his troops (PE, 148).

Phase V now begins. Upon its return from Egypt to Israel, the Russian army is devastated by the Europeans under the command of the Roman Antichrist. This devastation was predicted in Ezekiel 38:18-22 and 39:3-5.

> The description of torrents of fire and brimstone raining down upon the Red Army, coupled with an unprecedented shaking of the land of Israel could well be describing the use of tactical nuclear weapons against them by the Romans (PE, 149).

Ezekiel 39:6 also speaks of "fire": "I will send fire on Magog." This may refer either to a direct judgment from God, or to something that God allows man to do, such as an exchange of nuclear missiles (PE, 150).

The Battle of Armageddon

Finally the great conflict at Armageddon is waged.

> With the United Arab and African armies neutralized by the Russian invasion, and the consequent complete annihilation of the Russian forces and their homeland, we have only two great spheres of power left to fight the final climactic battle of Armageddon: the combined forces of the Western civilization united under the leadership of the Roman Dictator and the vast hordes of the Orient probably united under the Red Chinese war machine (PE, 151).

According to Lindsey (PE, 151), John predicts the mobilization of the Oriental powers: "And the sixth angel poured out his bowl upon the great river, the Euphrates; and its water was dried up, that the way might be prepared for the kings from the east" (Rev. 16:12 NASB). The Chinese lead this great army. They strike while the chaos of the Middle East conflict persists. Their opponent, the Roman dictator, prepares for battle by forcing the "kings of the whole world" to send their armies to fight under his command against the "kings from the east." He has no less than 200,000,000 soldiers when the two armies assemble at Armageddon.

Lindsey tells us that Armageddon refers to the great plain of Jezreel, which stretches across the Holy Land. The name *Armageddon* is derived from the Mount of Megiddo, located at one end of the plain. According to Lindsey, Napoleon is alleged to have stood on this mountain and said, "All the armies of the world could maneuver for battle here."

It will be a phenomenal battle:

> So here it is—the last great conflict. After the Antichrist assembles the forces of the rest of the whole world together, they meet the onrushing charge of the kings of the East in a battle line which will extend throughout Israel with the vortex centered at the Valley of Megiddo (PE, 154).

By referring to Zechariah 12:2-3 and 14:1-2, Lindsey claims that the terrible fighting will center around Jerusalem. So many people will be slaughtered that the prophecy of Revelation 14:20 will be fulfilled, namely, that the blood will form a shallow lake extending 200 miles north and south of Jerusalem. At that time the whole world will be leveled by earthquakes.

The Conversion of Israel and the Thousand-Year Reign

> As Armageddon begins with the invasion of Israel by the Arabs and the Russian confederacy, and their consequent swift destruction, the greatest period of Jewish conversion to their true Messiah will begin. Ezekiel predicts that the destruction of the great Russian invading force will have a supernatural element to it which will cause great numbers of Jews to see the hand of the Lord in it. Through the miraculous sign of the destruction of this enemy who sought to destroy all Jews they come to see the name of their true God and Messiah, Jesus Christ (PE, 156).

Lindsey likes to speak of Jesus as the Jewish Messiah. The time of the Great Tribulation is also called the Jewish period, because at that time God will put into action His special plan for the Jews. A great number of Jews will come to accept Jesus as their Messiah. This is indicated in Ezekiel 39:6-8 and in Zechariah 13:8-9.

The grand finale of the Battle of Armageddon will be the return of Christ to David's throne in Jerusalem. From there He will establish the Kingdom of God on earth, which is to last 1000 years (Rev. 20:4-6). Reference is also made to the prophecy of Isaiah 2:3-4, which "speaks of the time when the Messiah would reign over the earth out of Jerusalem and judge between the nations in a visible, actual, and historic Kingdom of God on earth" (PE, 158).

Lindsey labels his view a "premillennialist" position: "Those who believe that Christ will return and set up a 1000 year kingdom are called 'premillennialists' meaning Christ returns first, then establishes the kingdom on earth (PE, 164). The real issue, according to Lindsey, is whether the prophecies are to be interpreted literally or allegorically. He opts for the former method, according to which Christ will literally establish a kingdom that will last exactly 1000 years before it takes on the form of an eternal kingdom.

The critical question for Lindsey is: Does God keep His promises? Yes, says Lindsey. And this "yes" applies to the promise that God supposedly made to Abraham's descendants, namely, that they would rule over a worldwide kingdom through their Messiah, who would sit on David's throne. From Genesis 15:18-21, Lindsey gathers that the Jews who believe in the Messiah will possess the land bordered on the east by the Euphrates River and on the west by the Nile River: "It is promised that Jerusalem will be the spiritual center of the entire world and that all people of the earth will come annually to worship Jesus who will rule there" (PE, 165; see also Zech. 14:16-21; Is. 2:3; Mic. 4:1-3).

2

The Proper Method of Interpretation

"Literal" Interpretation?

It became evident at the end of the last chapter that Lindsey's manner of interpreting Scripture, notably the prophecies and the book of Revelation, is related to his premillennial point of view, according to which Christ will return to earth before He establishes His thousand-year kingdom. Lindsey opts for a literal interpretation of the prophecies. They tell us exactly what is going to happen. We today, living in the end times, experience the fulfillment of the prophecies.

Prophecy is meant to be read literally:

> The astonishing thing to those of us who have studied prophetic Scriptures is that we are watching the fulfillment of these prophecies in our time. Some of the future events that were predicted hundreds of years ago read like today's newspaper (PE, 10).

Lindsey cites the prophecies of Isaiah as an example. Isaiah prophesied what would happen in 100, 150, and

19

200 years, and it came to pass exactly as he had foretold it. The life of Jesus, the time, place and circumstances of His birth, His mission, His rejection and suffering, and His crucifixion all happened exactly as predicted by the prophets and psalmists.

Though many predictions were made about the *suffering* Messiah, even more predictions have been made about the *reigning* Messiah who is yet to come. These latter predictions are Lindsey's concern. In *The Late Great Planet Earth*, he wishes to "present the prophecies which are related to the specific pattern of world events which are precisely predicted as coming together shortly before the coming of the Messiah the second time—coming in power to rule the earth" (PE, 31).

Lindsey understands Christ's ruling of the earth to mean that He will rule on David's throne in Jerusalem during the thousand-year reign. The prophecies inform us of the events which will precede this reign. And so Lindsey reads literally the prophecies about Jerusalem, about David's throne, about Israel and the enemies which will confront Israel, and so forth. Since we live in the end times, shortly before the thousand-year reign, we are able to learn from the prophecies exactly what is going to happen on a global scale in the near future.

It is clear that this method of Scriptural interpretation arises out of the belief in the thousand-year kingdom. At the same time, this method of interpretation is bound up with a certain view of Israel, a view that stems from the premillennial stance. Notice what Lindsey says:

> The central theme of the Jewish prophets was that "the Messiah" would come and fulfill the promises given to their forefathers, Abraham, Isaac, and Jacob. In these promises Israel is to be the leading nation of the world

under the reign of the Messiah who would bring universal peace, prosperity, and harmony among all peoples of the earth (PE, 17-18).

In Chapter 4 we will discuss the thousand-year reign. Right now we wish to concern ourselves with the question of the would-be "literal" interpretation of prophecy. According to Lindsey, the Bible tells about the future; there are all sorts of unfulfilled prophecies which relate to the final period of history. We are able to map out this future period if we take all those prophetic fragments, lay them out like puzzle pieces, and fit them together in the proper manner to get a complete picture. Lindsey lifts pieces from all parts of the Bible—a prophecy of Daniel, a prediction of Jesus, a section of Revelation—and forces them together.

Lindsey proceeds in this manner because he believes it to be the role of the prophecies to give us insight into the future. This is his primary misconception. The prophecies were not given us in order that we might predict the future. A prophet is neither a soothsayer nor a fortune-teller but a herald of God's Word. A prophet proclaims the Word of the Lord.

That Word sometimes relates to the past, as when the prophet brings to light the true meaning and significance of historical events. The prophetic Word can also relate to the present, in the sense that it warns of sin and announces judgment. For example, God told Ezekiel: "Son of man, I have made you a watchman for the house of Israel" (Ezek. 3:17). And finally, the prophets very often deal with the future.

But with respect to the prophecies dealing with the future, we must realize that they were not given as a means for us to calculate the future. The Biblical prophecies aren't designed to give us a glimpse of the details of God's plan for the end times. The Kingdom of God is not subject to our calculations.

We used the phrase "the end times." Lindsey reads the Old Testament prophets and the book of Revelation as a description of such a future time, as a kind of eschatological blueprint. He neglects the fact that the prophets spoke primarily to the people of their time. They had a message for the contemporary generation of God's people. It is true that the message often related to the future. But it was a future that was tied to the situation of the covenant people of that time.

The Old Testament prophecies were often promises of redemption, namely, that the Lord would bring about a change in the fortunes of God's people. A closer look at these prophecies reveals that many of them bear on the return of Israel out of captivity. But this observation in no way exhausts such a promise of redemption. A further stage in its fulfillment is to be found in the coming of Jesus Christ, His birth, His death, and His resurrection. A third stage can often be seen in the establishment and expansion of the Church throughout the world. Such a prophecy of redemption is definitely fulfilled when Christ returns and the Church, gathered from among all peoples and all generations, shares fully in God's salvation in the New Jerusalem.

If we neglect this character of Biblical prophecy, we may come to some very bizarre conclusions, such as that Ezekiel prophesied about Russia, and Daniel about an Arab-African power of the twentieth century, and the book of Revelation about a Chinese power which would play a role in this century in the struggle against Israel. If we force together all these jigsaw pieces of Biblical prophecy, claiming in this way to map out the Biblical prophecies about the future, then we have completely misunderstood Scripture.

Certainly, God rescues Israel and destroys the enemy; this theme occurs repeatedly in the prophecies. But then we must neither look at an "Israel" of the "end times" nor at the modern nations. No, we need to focus on what Israel was at that time, namely, God's people, the Church of the old dispensation. It is to *that* Israel that God gives His promises of restoration and of the destruction of His enemies.

Only when we are clear about this can we follow prophecy through to its fulfillment in the New Testament era. There is much more to those Biblical prophecies about the future. When we unpack that "more," we must not forget that a prophecy about a time that was yet to come is rendered in the colors of the Old Testament period. Even though a prophecy about the redemption of God's people relates to more than Israel's deliverance from captivity, that "more" is still indicated in terms of the national character of the Church of the old dispensation.

In this connection we need to point out the compressed character of the prophetic prediction, or, as we might say, its telescopic character. We mean by this that the various events of a prophecy may be placed right next to each other in the prophecy while they are separated by centuries in their fulfillment. When we view a distant scene, a mountain may appear to rise directly behind the church steeple, but in reality the two are miles apart. As one writer expressed it: "Prophecy can be compared to a painting of a certain landscape, in which the houses, walking paths, and bridges of the foreground can be clearly distinguished, whereas the valleys and hills of the background, in reality separated from each other by great distances, are crowded next to each other."

In a similar fashion, there are no distinctions of time in the perspective of the prophets: judgment is one

judgment, and salvation is one salvation, even though the
later fulfillments occur at different points in time.

When the prophets announce the one great day of
the Lord, we should not think immediately of the final
judgment of the whole world, even though the prophecy
alludes to it. We must realize that the prophets saw the
day of the Lord first and foremost as the judgment that
was rapidly approaching, namely, the judgment of
Babylon and Assyria, of Edom or Moab, and also the
judgment of Israel. In those events we see the coming of
the Lord, the coming of His day. That coming finds its
ultimate fulfillment in the large-scale world judgment.

The prophets conceived of God's actions as a unity.
God's work is one work, whether it concerns judgment or
redemption. The oneness of redemption is shown by the
fact that the deliverance in Christ is proclaimed in connection with the deliverance from captivity. The lines often cross each other; no clear-cut distinctions are made
between the first and second coming of Christ, nor between the judgment of Babylon and the final judgment. A
prophecy about the coming and mission of Christ is
sometimes described in terms in which the final redemption becomes visible. A prophecy about Babylon may
contain nuances of the world judgment. We, who live in
the light of the New Testament fulfillment, can discern
those aspects of the prophecies which have already been
fulfilled. Those aspects which have not yet come to pass
must be understood in terms of Christ, His first coming to
the earth, His redemptive work, and the gathering of His
Church, which continues to the end of the world.

We wish to make several observations by referring
concretely to two prophetic predictions, the first being

Joel 3. Lindsey quotes from this prophecy in the section entitled "The Valley of Decision." He is referring to the "Valley of Jehoshaphat," where God gathers the nations so that He can judge them there.

Lindsey reads this prophecy in the following manner:

> Joel reveals that it is in this very place that the Messiah will destroy the armies of the world and establish his kingdom of true peace and everlasting happiness. He also confirms the world-wide assemblage of armies there.
>
> It is extremely important to note the accuracy of Bible prophecy in relation to this last conflict. In this day of H-bombs and super weapons, it seems incredible that there would ever be another great land war fought by basically conventional means (PE, 153).

Lindsey goes on to describe a Chinese force of 200,000,000 soldiers, who (according to yet another prophecy, Revelation 16:12) will advance by land. A road is already being built which would give the Chinese troops a short cut from Tibet to the subcontinent. When that road is completed, it will be possible for the millions of Chinese soldiers to advance quickly to the Middle East.

This is a good example of an (apparently) "literal" interpretation. We are immediately struck by the fact that the prophecy is forthwith related to the "end times," and in such a way that center stage is given not to Christ and His Church but to the Old Testament "Israel," which finds itself in the Middle East at that time. The whole history of redemption is ignored; there is no progression from the Old to the New Testament, no fulfillment of the old covenant in the new covenant. No thought is given to the concrete situation of the captivity, plunder, and exploitation of Israel, to which the prophecy of Joel 3 certainly does relate. No, Lindsey simply makes a giant leap to the Israel of the end times.

The Bible itself rules out any such "literal" interpretation. Indeed, Joel 3 begins with the words: "For behold, in those days and at that time . . . ." This relates to the end of Joel 2, where we find the Pentecost prophecy quoted by Peter in Acts 2:

> And it shall come to pass afterward, that I will pour out my spirit on all flesh . . . . And I will give portents in the heavens and on the earth, blood and fire and columns of smoke. The sun shall be turned to darkness, and the moon to blood, before the great and terrible day of the Lord comes. And it shall come to pass that all who call upon the name of the Lord shall be delivered; for in Mount Zion and in Jerusalem there shall be those who escape, as the Lord has said, and among the survivors shall be those whom the Lord calls (Joel 2:28, 30-2 RSV).

If we reflect on Peter's words in Acts 2, we might hear him saying: "Joel's prophecy, which was to be 'in the last days,' is now fulfilled. Those days have now begun, in that the Holy Spirit has been poured out.[1] The other signs, the blood, fire, and vapor of smoke, are on their way. The outpouring of the Holy Spirit has ushered in 'the great and terrible day of the Lord.'"

The prophecy of Joel 3 therefore bears on the era of Pentecost. It is about the Pentecost Church, about the body of Christ which is being gathered and which the

---

1. When we study prophecies about the "end times," we must remember that the Scriptures refer to the New Testament dispensation as "the last days" (Acts 2:17), "these last days" (Heb. 1:2), "the end of the ages" (I Cor. 10:11), and "the end of all things" (I Pet. 4:7).

unbelievers continue to assault. It is not about Israel in the end times but about the Church, which since Pentecost is the Church of the end of the ages.

When Joel speaks of "Jerusalem," we must understand this in New Testament terms as the body of believers on whom the Holy Spirit is poured out since Pentecost. Joel 2:1 explains the deliverance on Mount Zion and at Jerusalem of the preceding verse (2:32), in that God is going to destroy all the heathen nations.

In his Pentecost sermon Peter quotes Joel up to and including the words: "And it shall be that whoever calls on the name of the Lord shall be saved" (Acts 2:21 RSV). But according to Joel's prophecy, that salvation or deliverance was to be found on Mount Zion and at Jerusalem. Peter seems to have been well aware of the need for clarification, for at the end of his sermon he calls for disassociation from the Jewish religion with the same word "save": "Save yourselves from this crooked generation" (Acts 2:40 RSV). Salvation was not to be found in the Jewish synagogue or temple but in the upper room in Jerusalem, where the believers in Christ gathered together.

But we still need to ask ourselves: How are we to concretely understand the message of Joel 3? To do this we must first look at the concrete historical setting in which Joel lived and prophesied. Joash, the king of Judah, had just begun to rule. The Philistines and the Arabs had plundered Jerusalem not long before, during the rule of King Jehoram. They had taken many valuable treasures out of the palace and the temple and had dragged away many captives to be used as slaves. After dividing the booty by lot, they bartered it away for peanuts: a prostitute was paid with a Jewish boy, and a bottle of wine was exchanged for a Jewish girl. And so these Jews fell into the hands of the notorious slave dealers of that time, the Philistines and the Phoenicians, who resold them to the Ionians or Greeks.

The Lord will not allow this state of affairs. He assembles all nations in the valley of Jehoshaphat in order to enter into judgment with them "on account of my people and my heritage Israel, because they have scattered them among the nations" (Joel 3:2-3 RSV).

One might ask: Doesn't Joel exaggerate here? He speaks of all the nations, but weren't the Philistines, the Arabs, and the Phoenicians the only ones involved? Wasn't it a little far-fetched to say that God's people and heritage Israel was "scattered among the nations"?

Joel has in mind a larger picture: he is referring to the hatred of all nations against Israel, or against the Church after Pentecost. Joel is looking at the whole history of the Church, from beginning to end. He sees how the Lord unites the unbelievers in their hatred against the Church, so that He can enter into judgment with them. He gathers them in the valley of Jehoshaphat, which means *valley of judgment*, so that He can judge them in the shadow of Jerusalem, in the shadow of the Church.

And so the Lord brings about a change in the fortunes of Jerusalem and ends the humiliation of His people. Joel prophesies that the day of the Lord in the valley of decision is near. At that time the sun and the moon will be darkened, and the stars will cease to shine. The Lord will roar from Zion and lift His voice from Jerusalem, so that heaven and earth shake (Joel 3:14ff). Those events remind us of the Pentecost prophecy at the end of Joel 2. Joel is concerned with the day of the Lord that began with Pentecost and will be concluded with Christ's return.

The end of Joel 3 once again presents the contrast: the relief to be found in Judah and Jerusalem, as opposed to the felling of the heathen nations by judgment. Joel uses prophetic-poetic language to sketch the rich blessings that Judah will enjoy. These blessings proceed from the presence of the Lord, "for the Lord dwells in Zion."

This method of interpretation does justice to the character of the Old Testament prophecy, because it takes the following into account:

a) the concrete historical situation from which the prophet spoke,
b) the relationship with the history of redemption and therefore with the New Testament,
c) the national framework of the prophecy,
d) the prophetic perspective with respect to "the day of the Lord."

In this way we "compare Scripture with Scripture," which is principially different from fitting together pieces of a jigsaw puzzle, as Hal Lindsey's method would have it.

It will be instructive to take a brief look at a second prophecy, namely, the well-known prophecy of Isaiah 9:1-2. It reads:

> But there will be no gloom for her that was in anguish. In the former time he brought into contempt the land of Zebulun and the land of Naphtali, but in the latter time he will make glorious the way of the sea, the land beyond the Jordan, Galilee of the nations. The people who walked in darkness have seen a great light; those who dwelt in a land of deep darkness, on them has light shined (RSV).

This is a prophecy of redemption concerning the northern section of the country: the territory of Zebulun and Naphtali, which formed the larger part of what was later known as Galilee. According to Isaiah, the Lord had brought this area into contempt in a former time. The great promise of this prophecy stands out clearly against the somber background of the wretched past of Zebulun and Naphtali. These two tribes shared a long history of apostasy. When Israel was conquered by Assyria as punishment for her sins, a catastrophe befell the area under discussion: the Assyrians carried away captive most of the population of Galilee and Naphtali (II Kings 15:27-31). And so they were thrust in darkness (Is.8:20-21).

But then Isaiah comes with the prophecy of redemption. The people walked in darkness, that is to say, they endured great misery, not just on account of the Assyrian conquest but also on account of their sin and apostasy. God comes to that people with a great light.

This does refer to the fact that this people will be freed from Assyrian oppression in the near future. "For the yoke of his burden, and the staff for his shoulder, the rod of his oppressor, thou has broken as on the day of Midian" (Is. 9:4 RSV). But there is more to the prophecy: the people will be freed from sin by the Messiah who is coming and who will sit eternally on David's throne. This is an example of the compressed character of prophecy in that the Messianic salvation is described in the same breath as the end of the Assyrian oppression.

But there is more to be said. Matthew writes that Jesus, upon learning of the arrest of John, withdrew into Galilee. He left Nazareth and went to live in Capernaum by the sea, in the territory of Zebulun and Naphtali (Matt. 4:12-13). This geographical location of Capernaum makes Matthew think of the Messianic prophecy of Isaiah 8:23—9:2, which refers to this area in which Capernaum is located as the future field of activity of the promised Messiah. Matthew connects this move to Capernaum with the fulfillment of Isaiah's prophecy:

> . . . that what was spoken by the prophet Isaiah might be fulfilled: "The land of Zebulun and the land of Naphtali, toward the sea, across the Jordan, Galilee of the Gentiles—the people who sat in darkness have seen a great light, and for those who sat in the region and shadow of death light has dawned" (Matt. 4:14-16 RSV).

Of what does this dawning of light consist? Matthew immediately makes that clear: "From that time Jesus began to preach, saying, 'Repent, for the kingdom of heaven is at hand.' " The fulfillment of the prophecy is found in His preaching throughout Galilee. The move to Capernaum was not the actual fulfillment, but it made the fulfillment possible in that Jesus would then make the territory of Zebulun and Naphtali His field of activity.

It is in this way that Zebulun and Naphtali figure in the prophecy. It is clearly evident that Isaiah's prophecy does not refer to a future, national kind of glory for the territory of Galilee. The New Testament points us in a very different direction—to the preaching of Jesus in that area.

But He is no longer there. He has gone on, from Capernaum to Jerusalem and Golgotha. After His resurrection He preceded the disciples to Galilee, but He did not remain there. He went on to Bethany and to the Mount of Olives, from where He ascended into heaven, and now He sits at the right hand of the Father. That is where His throne is, according to the prophecy of Isaiah 9:7: "Of the increase of his government and of peace there will be no end, upon the throne of David, and over his kingdom . . . ." Today that Kingdom of peace is not limited to Galilee, but extends to all places where Christ is gathering His Church, and it will have no limits when Christ returns. That event will be the complete fulfillment of Isaiah's prophecy.

"In the Latter Days"

One may still ask: Don't the prophets often speak about what will occur "in the latter days"? Aren't they referring to what will happen in the final period of history? Isn't it true that such a prophecy about the end times is tied up with the prophecy of the restoration of Israel and of David's kingdom?

We will not avoid these questions. We will discuss the various places in the Old Testament where the expression "in the latter days" occurs. It appears thirteen times: Genesis 49:1; Numbers 24:14; Deuteronomy 4:30; 31:29; Isaiah 2:2; Jeremiah 23:20; 30:24; 48:47; 49:39; Ezekiel 38:16; Daniel 2:28; 10:14; Hosea 3:5; and Micah 4:1 (see also Isaiah 2:2).

In Genesis 49:1 we read: "Then Jacob called his sons, and said, 'Gather yourselves together, that I may tell you what shall befall you *in days to come*.' "[2] Thus begins the parting speech of the dying Jacob to his sons.

"In days to come" or "in the latter days" in this

---

2. In two of the thirteen instances of the Hebrew phrase *be'acharit hayamim*, the English (Revised Standard) version has rendered it "in the days to come," rather than "in the latter days."—TRANS.

passage refers first of all to the time immediately after Jacob's death, in which his sons will continue to live after him. It also refers to the time of the tribes of Israel. Jacob's words to Judah even indicate the coming of the Messiah, which is the only regard in which Jacob's prophecy reaches beyond the bounds of the Old Testament: "The scepter shall not depart from Judah, nor the ruler's staff from between his feet, until he comes to whom it belongs; and to him shall be the obedience of the peoples" (Gen. 49:10 RSV).

We may conclude that "in the latter days" refers to the time of Jacob's descendants, the tribes or nation of Israel; only once does it refer to the New Testament appearance of the Messiah. We certainly have no reason to interpret the expression in this passage to mean the final period of world history.

We next find the expression "in the latter days" at the beginning of the fourth oracle of Balaam, in Numbers 24:14: "And now, behold, I am going to my people; come, I will let you know what this people will do to your people *in the latter days*." The fortune-teller Balaam will then tell the frightened king of Moab what he can expect at the hand of the people of Israel. To which time in the future is he referring? Balaam's words give us a clue: "I see him, but not now; I behold him, but not nigh: a star shall come forth out of Jacob, and a scepter shall rise out of Israel; it shall crush the forehead of Moab, and break down all the sons of Sheth" (Num. 24:17 RSV).

It is very tempting to read the words *star* and *scepter* as direct references to Christ, especially in connection with Genesis 49:10 and Revelation 22:16. But it has been correctly pointed out that while Christ lived on earth He

had no army at His disposal, nor did He have anything to
do with the destruction of Moab. But doesn't Balaam
foresee Christ's coming to the earth? Yes, he does, but not
in a direct sense. He sees a royal figure who humiliates
Moab within the context of the Old Testament and its
political realities. This is an allusion to *David*, who
crushed the Moabites and made them tribute-paying sub-
jects (II Sam. 8:2). The theocracy of David and of his
successors heralded the coming of Christ, who would
bring about a perfect kingdom.

Here again we find that several aspects of the future
are compressed together: the concrete historical situation
of David's kingdom, the coming of Christ, and the per-
fection of His Kingdom. They are all contained in the
prediction of what Israel will do to Moab "in the latter
days." It is obvious that this expression does not refer,
either directly or exclusively, to the end of the world.

In Deuteronomy 4:30 we read: "When you are in
tribulation, and all these things come upon you *in the latter days*, you will return to the Lord your God and obey
his voice." It is not difficult to determine here which
period of time is indicated by the expression "in the latter
days." In the preceding verses (25-8) we learn of the sentences which God will mete out to the Israelites if they
forsake the Lord and lapse into idolatry and the worship
of images. Moses makes this clear to God's people of that
time:

> When you beget children and children's children,
> and have grown old in the land, if you act corruptly
> by making a graven image in the form of anything,
> and by doing what is evil in the sight of the Lord

your God . . . the Lord will scatter you among the peoples, and you will be left few in number among the nations where the Lord will drive you (Deut. 4:25-7 RSV).

The latter days are therefore the time in which Israel is scattered among the peoples on account of her sin. This refers to the Assyrian and Babylonian captivity, which the Scriptures often indicate with the expression "scatter among the nations."[3] Again, there is no reference to the final chapter of world history.

The same is true of Deuteronomy 31:29. Moses says to the Israelites:

For I know that after my death you will surely act corruptly; and turn aside from the way which I have commanded you; and in *the days to come*[4] evil will befall you, because you will do what is evil in the sight of the Lord, provoking him to anger through the work of your hands.

The evil that will befall Israel is the punishment of her apostasy. It is the same evil that was described in Deuteronomy 4:26-8. Moses again described it in detail in Deuteronomy 28:15ff. Here again, therefore, "in the latter days" does not refer to the end of the world.

We now come to the well-known prophecy of Isaiah 2:2-4 about the migration of the nations to Jerusalem.

3. See I Kings 14:15; Nehemiah 1:8; Psalm 44:11; Jeremiah 9:16; 16:15; 23:8; 30:11; 31:10; Ezekiel 11:16; 12:15.

4. See footnote 2 of this chapter.

It shall come to pass in the latter days that the mountain of the house of the Lord shall be established as the highest of the mountains, and shall be raised above the hills; and all the nations shall flow to it, and many peoples shall come, and say: "Come, let us go up to the mountain of the Lord, to the house of the God of Jacob; that he may teach us his ways and that we may walk in his paths." For out of Zion shall go forth the law, and the word of the Lord from Jerusalem. He shall decide for many peoples; and they shall beat their swords into ploughshares, and their spears into pruning hooks; nation shall not lift up sword against nation, neither shall they learn war any more (RSV).

The same prophecy is found in Micah 4:1. Biblical scholars disagree as to whether Isaiah or Micah is the original author of the prophecy. Suffice it to say that strong arguments point to Isaiah's being the original author.

In this prophecy Jerusalem does not function as a political center of power but as the central place of worship. It is a cultic center for the peoples who seek instruction in the law of God. The nations will go there "in the latter days." This does not take place in the time of Isaiah, nor in the later period of Israel's history. This prophecy refers beyond the Old Testament to the New Testament dispensation when Christ comes. His coming is the keynote of the completion of all things, and it ushers in the end of the ages.

When Isaiah mentions "the mountain of the house of the Lord," he is speaking of Mount Zion, upon which the temple was located. Mount Zion was God's chosen dwelling place. His presence there in the middle of His people brought blessing and salvation. Isaiah prophesies that all nations will flock to this towering Mount Zion where Yahweh dwells. They flock there because they want to be where the Lord lives: "Come, let us go up to the mountain of the Lord, to the house of the God of Jacob."

Redemption would become universal, offered to all people. For centuries Israel had enjoyed the privilege of being God's special covenant people, but soon salvation would be offered to all peoples, according to Christ's command in Matthew 28:19. At that time the heathen nations would participate in the redemption of "the God of Jacob" along with the converted Israelites.

The name *God of Jacob* reminds us that it was not even a matter of course that Israel participated in God's redemption. Jacob was chosen to be the ancestor of the people of Israel, but not on account of his own efforts (however much he did try). Rather, it was God's pleasure to show His grace to Jacob. And now, in the latter days, God also shows His grace to the non-Israelites.

The prophecy is again couched in Old Testament terms. It is to Mount Zion, to the temple, that the heathen nations will come. But this clearly has a New Testament significance: the house of the God of Jacob overflows as the Gentiles converge on Jerusalem. The Gentiles want the Lord to teach them His ways, and they want to walk in His paths. They wish to understand the will of Yahweh, because peace and salvation are to be found only in obedience to that will.

This prophecy is in sharp contrast with the events of the time of Isaiah. The Assyrian kingdom was rising in power. In its conquest of the nations, its armies even reached the gates of Jerusalem. It was engaged in building a universal empire. But God's plan calls for different events. He draws the peoples to Jerusalem, from where He rules, and where His law and Word are to be found. A Kingdom of peace is coming, whose center will be Zion.

This is no reference to the final period of history, in which Christ will rule from Jerusalem. As we have said, Jerusalem must be seen here as a cultic center and not as a political center. Besides, the prophet is speaking in Old Testament terms. Jerusalem refers to the Church, in which all nations will be involved. All peoples will be brought together to form the one universal or catholic Church. They will form the one body of Christ, gathered out of all the nations. They will be like a spiritual house, according to I Peter 2:5.

This does not mean that the prophecy has been completely fulfilled. We are given a glimpse of a distant scene in the proclamation that nations will no longer use swords, nor learn the art of war. This proclamation from Isaiah is written on the United Nations building in New York. The whole world longs for this genuine peace.

But the human race cannot create the Kingdom of peace. That Kingdom can only come in and through Christ, who is already building it by gathering His Church out of all nations. Christ is bringing all races of people together to form one people. That work will not be completed until His return. At the end of the ages, Isaiah's prophecy about the migration of the nations to Jerusalem will finally be completely fulfilled: "Behold, the dwelling of God is with men. He will dwell with them, and they shall be his people, and God himself will be with them" (Rev. 21:3 RSV). Here the prophecy about "the latter days" reaches this far into the future.

What does Jeremiah mean by "the latter days"? In Jeremiah 23:20, and in an almost identical verse (Jer. 30:24), the prophet describes the fierce anger of God that will break loose over the wicked. His anger will not abate until He has fully carried out His plan, in which the enemy from the north (the Chaldeans) will crush the sinful nation. Then Jeremiah continues with: "*In the latter days* you will understand it clearly."

Until now the people had turned a deaf ear to the prophetic warnings of judgment. But when that judgment finally came, they would realize how mistaken they had been, and they would admit their foolishness. This would happen in "the latter days," which are not the final period of history but the time when God's judgment would result in the destruction of Jerusalem and the deportation into captivity.

Jeremiah refers to "the latter days" when he prophesies about how the Lord will restore the fortunes of Moab (Jer. 48:47) and those of Elam (Jer. 49:39). In these passages, "the latter days" suggests the end of a certain period, namely, the period in which God's vengeance strikes these nations. God will punish and destroy these nations, and then, "in the latter days," He will come to them also with redemption. This makes us think of a time beyond the old dispensation, a time when salvation extends to all nations. Grace will also be shown to Moab and to Elam. We may read verses such as these in connection with Jeremiah 3:17, which says that all nations will gather in Jerusalem (compare Is. 2:2ff). This happens in the era of Pentecost, when the Church is being gathered out of all the nations.

In Ezekiel 38:16, the expression "in the latter days" occurs in a prophecy about Gog. Opinions differ as to whether this prophecy bears directly on the end of times, or whether it refers to an event in the history of the Israel of the old covenant. (We will discuss this passage in detail in Chapter 8.)

In Daniel 2:28, Daniel says to King Nebuchadnezzar: "There is a God in heaven who reveals mysteries, and he has made known to King Nebuchadnezzar what will be *in the latter days.*" In his dream the king surveyed the world empires beginning with Nebuchadnezzar and ending with the Diadochian empires, at which time the Greek-Macedonian empire split. (This is discussed in more detail in Chapter 11.) Here the expression "in the latter days" does not refer to the end of the world but to the succession of various powers and world empires in the immediate future.

We also need to look at Daniel 10:14, in which the angel, who brings Daniel a vision from God, says to Daniel that he "came to make you understand what is to befall your people *in the latter days.*" The vision (Dan. 11:2ff) gives an overview of what would happen from Cyrus to Antiochus Epiphanes; the largest part of the vision deals with the appearance of the latter. (See Chapter 9 for a further discussion of Antiochus Epiphanes.) The angel says to Daniel that he has come to make him understand what is to befall "*your* people" because God's people suffered under Antiochus Epiphanes. "The latter days" refers to this period of suffering which lay in the distant future at the time of Daniel. It does not mean the time just before the end of the world.

One might argue that the resurrection of the dead in Daniel 12:2 undoubtedly does take place at the end of the world. But we need to keep in mind that the resurrection of the dead is seen here in relation to the severe persecution that the Jewish people endured under Antiochus Epiphanes. According to Daniel 12:1, great trouble will come at that time. "At that time" refers to the previously described period of Antiochus's rule. But then we read the message of comfort, first that there will be deliverance for the living (end of vs. 1), and secondly that there will be a resurrection for those who perished during the terrible persecution. At the same time a warning is given for the benefit of the unbelievers, who will awake "to shame and everlasting contempt."

There remains one last passage of Scripture to be discussed in this context, namely, Hosea 3:5: "Afterward the children of Israel shall return and seek the Lord their God, and David their king; and they shall come in fear to the Lord and to his goodness *in the latter days.*"

The same time period is indicated by "afterward" and "in the latter days." The events of verse 5 will take place after the time when Israel shall dwell many days without king or prince, without sacrifice or pillar, without ephod or teraphim (vs. 4). In other words, Israel will be without government and religion during the time of the captivity, which will last "many days."

The punishment will produce a change in attitude. The children of Israel will return to the Lord. They will seek Yahweh their God and David their king. They will come trembling with distress about their sins. But they will also tremble with the joy born of God's boundless mercy. Therefore "in the latter days" first of all refers to the time of the return from captivity.

What is meant by the seeking of "David their king"? In the first instance it indicates the events mentioned in Hosea 1:11: the people of Judah and the people of Israel come together to appoint one head over themselves. The ruler will be a king from David's line. When we think of it in this way, "Israel" indicates the ten northern tribes who now once again become subject to the kings of David's family.

But we have not yet finished interpreting this

passage. Another nuance of the text comes to the fore what we study its parallelism. The people seek the Lord their God and David their king, and they come to the Lord and His goodness. The first objects in each clause correspond to each other, and so do the second. Therefore "David their king" corresponds to "His goodness." God will show His goodness to Israel in the return of David their king, which will occur when the Messiah comes.

It is a mistake to think of the turning to the Lord and to David as the conversion of the Jews, in the final period of history, to a Messiah who sits on an actual throne in Jerusalem. The source of blessing is the Lord—not the throne of David. Other passages make this clear. In Jeremiah 31:12, the goodness of the Lord is the source of all blessings, which include grain, wine, oil, and so forth. This verse echoes Hosea 2:21ff. The passage in question, Hosea 3:5, is analogous to Amos 9:11-15, where God first raises up the fallen house of David and then bestows blessings upon the land.

We have no reason, then, to interpret the reference to "David" in a national, Jewish sense. The New Testament shows us the richer fulfillment of these prophecies. During the conference of church leaders at Jerusalem, James quotes the prophecy about the restoration of the fallen house of David (Amos 9:11-12). With this text he wishes to show that "God first visited the Gentiles, to take out of them a people for his name" (Acts 15:14 RSV).

In Romans 9:25-6, Paul refers to Hosea 2:22 and 1:10: "Those who were not my people I will call 'my people,' and her who was not beloved I will call 'my beloved.' And in the very place where it was said to them, 'You are not my people,' they will be called 'sons of the living God!' " Paul quotes Hosea in order to prove that God calls His children not only from among the Jews, but also from among the Gentiles.

Therefore the goodness of the Lord that Israel experiences at the time of "David their king" in the latter days refers to the goodness that the Lord who sits on David's throne presently shows to His Church, which is composed of Jews and Gentiles.

We can end this discussion about the expression "in the latter days" by concluding that it certainly is not synonymous with "in the final period of history." The only generalization that we can make is that the expression refers to the future. We can ascertain the actual time period in the future that is indicated only from the passage and its context. Often "in the latter days" indicates the time of the return from captivity, and sometimes, in addition, it indicates the time of the Messiah, and possibly even the time when the world will end. In certain cases the expression refers directly to the time of the Messiah. But in none of the passages does the expression "in the latter days" refer directly to the final period of world history.

3

The Prophecy of the Book of Revelation

The book of Revelation is the revelation of Jesus Christ (Rev. 1:1). It describes itself as a prophecy, in the first chapter (vs. 3) as well as in the last chapter (vs. 7, 10, 18, 19,).

The book of Revelation, like all prophecy, relates to the past, present and future. It sheds light on the past, for example, in the vision of chapter 12, where the dragon stands ready to devour the child of the woman as soon as it is born. The woman represents God's people throughout their Old Testament history, and the dragon represents satan, who during all those centuries tried to prevent the coming of the promised seed of the woman, the Messiah. An example of prophecy concerning the present is found in the description of the contemporary seven churches of Asia in chapters 2 and 3.

However, this last book of the Bible contains mostly prophecy about the future. John was given the following task: "Write down therefore what you have seen, what is now, and what will be hereafter" (Rev. 1:19 NEB). John describes what he "has seen" in chapter 1: the glorious appearance of Jesus Christ, who died but now lives. The seven churches of Asia (ch. 2-3) are "what is now." The

44

rest of Revelation concerns itself with "what will be hereafter." In Revelation 4:1 the angel says to John: "I will show you what must take place after this," that is to say, what will take place after the things described in the seven letters to the churches.

The prophecy concerning the future in Revelation deals with the coming of the Lord Jesus Christ. This is clear early in the book: "Behold, he is coming with the clouds, and every eye will see him" (1:7), and again at the end of the book, when Christ Himself says, "I am coming soon" (22:7, 12, 20).

This does not mean that Revelation only concerns itself with the appearance of the Lord Jesus on the clouds on the last day. Nor is it merely concerned with the happenings of a final period of history just before Christ's return. Rather, Revelation embraces the whole New Testament era, from Christ's ascension and the outpouring of the Holy Spirit, with which the "latter days" were ushered in (Acts 2:17), to the time of His return. The coming of the Lord Jesus Christ takes place during the whole period from Christ's ascension to the moment of His reappearance.

The book of Revelation is carefully structured: seven seals, seven trumpets, and seven bowls. The judgments of God strike the earth when the seals are opened, the trumpets are blown, and the bowls are emptied. The Lord Jesus comes into His glory throughout the New Testament era by way of the judgments.

The seals, trumpets and bowls are closely interrelated. The seventh seal results in seven trumpets, and the seventh trumpet results in seven bowls. This does not mean that the seven seals, trumpets, and bowls are themselves consecutive.[1] Each series traces the historical

---

1. See Klaas Schilder, *De Openbaring van Johannes en het sociale leven* (Delft, 1951), p. 129.

period from Christ's ascension to His return, but each time in a different light. When the seventh seal is opened, we are very close to the end of history. But we do not see the end, because the blowing of the first trumpet takes us back to the beginning. When the seventh trumpet is blown, we are once again near the end, but must return to the beginning with the vision of the seven bowls. In this manner we traverse the centuries several times.

Each series of seven involves an intensification of judgment. The judgment of the fourth seal affects one fourth of the earth (Rev. 6:8). The blowing of the trumpets destroys one third of the earth (Rev. 8:7-12; 9:15, 18). Finally, the outpouring of God's wrath from the seven bowls devastates the whole world. This time everything is ravaged—the earth and the people (16:2), the sea and every living thing in the sea (vs. 3), the rivers and springs (vs. 4), the people (vs. 8-9), the cities (vs. 19), and every island (vs. 20).

There is a definite structure to the judgments of God, just as there is a structure to the unfolding of history, which happens according to God's plan. We would do well to remember that God does not allow us a complete knowledge of His plan. In Revelation 10:4 we learn that it is God's will for us not to know everything that will happen. John writes, "And when the seven thunders had sounded, I was about to write, but I heard a voice from heaven saying, 'Seal up what the seven thunders have said, and do not write it down.' " It is therefore clear that the book of Revelation does not equip us to map out the whole future, that it does not present the history of the future.

The description of "what will be hereafter" begins in

chapter 4 with a description of the heavenly throne panorama. John sees the Lord God sitting on His throne with the sealed scroll of chapter 5 in His right hand. No one was able to open the seven seals of the scroll. In this way the Bible tells us that no human being is able to know God's plan and carry it out.

When John weeps about this, one of the elders directs him to look at Christ, the Lion of the tribe of Judah and the Root of David. Because He has conquered, He is able to open the scroll and break the seals. John sees Him as the Lamb by the throne, the Lamb that was slain, who had shed His blood and conquered satan. He is worthy to open the scroll and carry out God's decrees.

Although Christ conquered satan in principle on the cross of Golgotha, the struggle between these two, which is the stuff of world history, still continues, and will continue until satan is thrown into the lake of fire (Rev. 20:10).

The point of world history does not lie in people or earthly powers. The decisions are made not on earth but in heaven, where Christ rules out of the power of His sacrifice. The cross of Golgotha stands at the center of history. The book of Revelation shows us that Christ is winning, and that His Kingdom is coming with glory.

The Lamb takes the scroll out of God's right hand (5:7) and opens the seven seals (6:1ff). On account of His sacrifice on Golgotha, Christ is able to set God's plan in motion.

The breaking of six of the seven seals in chapter 6[2]

---

2. On Revelation 6:1—8:6, see Holwerda, *De wijsheid die behoudt* (Goes, 1957), pp. 194-223.

sends war, revolution, hunger, and epidemic into the world.[3] When the fifth seal is opened, John sees under the altar the souls of those who were slain for the Word of God and for the witness they bore. They were martyrs for the gospel of Christ. They were killed because the Word of God acted as their witness in the great lawsuit. In John's vision they cry out, "Why don't You uphold Your witness by avenging our blood?" Then they are comforted and told that their sacrifice has been accepted, and that their blood has been received on the altar of God. God postpones His vengeance so that His grace may triumph. New witnesses must still appear so that the number of God's servants will be complete.

The opening of the sixth seal results in a great earthquake and the disintegration of the universe. And so we have passed from events which recur during the whole New Testament dispensation to the events of the final judgment. The great day of God's wrath has come. Who can stand before it?

The events of chapter 7 form another part of the opening of the sixth seal. The visions of chapter 7 are closely connected with the end of chapter 6, where John heard the question: Who can stand before it? The answer is: The 144,000 out of all the tribes of the children of Israel, who have a seal on their foreheads showing that they belong to God. They will be saved when the universe is demolished.

The number 144,000 has a symbolic meaning: 144,000 = 12 x 12 x 1,000. The number 12 symbolizes

---

3. Many Reformed exegetes, including S. Greijdanus and K. Schilder see the rider of the white horse as Christ or the gospel. In our opinion there is a good case to be made instead for seeing all four riders as independent powers of judgment. See Holwerda, *De wijsheid die behoudt*, pp. 198ff, for the details of this discussion.

that the New Testament church has the same character of completion that the 12 tribes gave to Israel of the Old Testament. The number 1,000 stands for a huge number, an immense multitude. Therefore the number of those who will be able to stand will be the complete, great number that God has determined.

In the next scene, John sees a great, triumphant multitude standing before the throne and the Lamb. This vision shows him how God's promise is actually being fulfilled: the full number of the huge crowd is being rescued and gathered throughout the ages, until all things are completed. The Feast of Tabernacles continues to be fulfilled in the gathering of the Church (see Zech. 14:16ff).

The opening of the seventh seal in chapter 8 causes a half hour of silence in heaven. Then the seal unfolds into seven trumpets, which are given to seven angels. The angels prepare to blow the trumpets. Heaven holds its breath. What is going to happen?

But the angels are not allowed to blow the trumpets until the prayers of the saints are brought to God in a censer. Then the judgments of the seven trumpets break out upon apostate humanity, and fire falls upon the earth. That fire is taken from the altar where the prayers of the saints are offered. The catastrophes that befall unbelieving humanity are answers to the prayers of the Church that God's name would be hallowed, and that His Kingdom would come. This means that the Church, no matter how weak she appears, possesses great strength through her prayers. Her prayers hasten the great day of salvation.

The rest of chapters 8 and 9 describes the judgments

that the blowing of the trumpets will loose upon the earth throughout the centuries.

The sixth trumpet is the prelude to the seven thunders. John sees a mighty angel descend from heaven with a little open scroll in his hand. His appearance is announced by the shattering sound of seven thunders. John is not allowed to write down the ominous content of the messages of the thunders. It remains a secret between Christ, who gives this revelation, and His servant John (Rev. 10:4).

The seven thunders also characterize something that embraces the course of history. However ominous the content of the claps of thunder, God's redemptive plan must still be put into effect, for Revelation 10:7 says that the mystery of God will be fulfilled at the time of the trumpet call by the seventh angel. And John has to eat the opened scroll because prophecy must continue.

The events of chapter 11 are still part of the sixth trumpet. This chapter is concerned with the whole New Testament era, which is first indicated by 42 months, and then by 1260 days. This era appears here in terms of the witness of the Church. We learn how God's witnesses have great influence on the course of events.

Chapter 11 tells us that God's witnesses have the power to shut the sky and to turn water into blood. Only after this has been driven home does the seventh trumpet sound, ushering in the end of world history.

Who are the two witnesses? Revelation 11:4 says: "These are the two olive trees and the two lampstands which stand before the Lord of the earth." This reminds us of Zechariah 4:11-14, in which the two olive trees represent "the two anointed who stand by the Lord of the whole earth." We are dealing here with the (anointed) of-fice-bearers of the Church, who represent the whole Church. The two servants of God in the passage from Zechariah may allude to Zerubbabel and Jeshua, who were contemporaries of Zechariah. The two witnesses of Revelation 11 are the representatives of Christ's wit-nesses, or of the church of the New Testament.

The fact that there are "two" witnesses not only reminds us of Zechariah 4 but also legitimizes their wit-ness, since every word confirmed by two witnesses was to be considered reliable.

The portrayal of the two witnesses also makes us think of Moses, who turned water into blood, and of Elijah, whose prayers shut the sky during the days of his prophetic work. The authorization that Christ's witnesses receive is just as great as that of Moses and Elijah. To-gether Christ's witnesses possess all power, whose source is faith and prayer. The writer of Hebrews speaks of Moses' miracles in Egypt in conjunction with his faith (Heb. 11:27). It was Elijah's prayers that warded off the rain (James 5:17-18).

This power of "the two witnesses" is not exercised in a visible, earthshaking manner. But it exists, never-theless. The spiritual energy of their faith and prayers en-sures that in spite of all calamities, the Church is being drawn out of the world, but also that the world is being drawn out of the Church. Moses did the former, and Elijah the latter.

The witnesses will continue their work until they have finished their testimony (Rev. 11:7). They come equipped with their prophecy, just as Christ their Lord did. And as He rose after His death and ascended to heaven, so they, after their death, will rise up and go to heaven. Christ lets them share in the first resurrec-tion (Rev. 20:4-6).

When the seventh trumpet is blown, John hears two hymns of praise to the kingship of the Lord and His Christ (Rev. 11:15, 17-18). This kingship is now going to reveal itself fully (11:19). Here we are close to the end of history, but once again, for the fourth time (after the seals, thunderclaps and trumpets), we get a view of all of history. This time the vision begins in the Old Testament (12:1ff) and proceeds to the New Testament era in the birth and ascension of Christ (12:5-6). With the ascension satan is thrown out of heaven, and after that he devotes himself to the persecution of the woman, or the body of Christ, on earth.

Two earthly powers assist satan in his work. The first, the beast out of the sea, is the ungodly political power that wages war with the Church for 42 months, i.e. during the whole New Testament era (13:1-10). The significance of this power will be discussed in Chapter 12. The second assistant is the beast out of the earth, who represents false prophecy, which lures the people on earth to kneel before the ungodly political power (13:11-18).

But the faithful believers remain true to the Lord and His Christ. God preserves His Church in the face of the fury of the "beasts." John has seen how the complete number, the 144,000, are assembled on Mount Zion, i.e. in the New Jerusalem (14:1-5). And so we once again approach the end of the world: the last judgment is announced (14:6-13), and a twofold harvest occurs—one for the heavenly granaries, and one for the winepress of God's wrath (14:14-20).

The seven angels appear with the seven last plagues (15:1), which again take us from the beginning to the end of history. With these plagues, "The wrath of God is ended." In this last outpouring of God's anger, the whole world collapses (16:1-21). In chapters 17 and 18, John describes the judgment of Babylon, the apostate Church, which perishes. (In Chapter 13 we will discuss this judgment in detail.) Only when Babylon has perished can the marriage supper of the Lamb begin. Then the beast and his propagandist, the false prophet, are thrown into the lake of fire.

Before we learn how satan perishes, chapter 20 gives a brief sketch of his history during the New Testament dispensation. He is bound for a thousand years, after which he is set free for a short time to mobilize the pagan forces against the Church. But then God intervenes. Fire comes down from heaven; the masses who have followed satan are consumed. Satan is thrown into the lake of fire and brimstone. (We will deal with the thousand years of satan's imprisonment in the next chapter.)

After satan has been completely done in, the final judgment occurs. The dead are resurrected; they are judged according to their works and thrown into the lake of fire. This second death does not touch those whose names are written in the book of life (20:11-15).

Chapters 21 and 22 describe the consummation. There is a new heaven and a new earth. The New Jerusalem descends out of heaven; within it the believers out of all nations exist in a state of absolute blessedness, because God dwells with His people (Rev. 21:3). In this way the ancient promise of God's dwelling with His people, made repeatedly to Israel of old, is finally fulfilled (see Lev. 26:11-22; Jer. 30:22; Ezek. 37:27; Zech. 8:8). A thousand-year reign in which Israel is the focal point does not fulfill this promise. Only when God gathers all peoples in the New Jerusalem is it fulfilled.

4

A Thousand-Year Reign

The Church Is No Interlude

Many people expect a thousand-year reign of peace on the basis of Revelation 20, which speaks of the binding of satan for one thousand years while the believers reign with Christ. The expectation is for a twofold return of Christ and a twofold resurrection.

With His first return, Christ will resurrect the believers, who will rule with Him as kings on the earth for a thousand years. Revelation 20:5 is cited as the basis for the belief in the first resurrection: "This is the first resurrection." With the second coming, all people, including the unbelievers, will rise from the dead.

This kingdom is supposed to last exactly 1000 years. Seated on the throne of David in Jerusalem, Christ will rule the earth for ten centuries. The temple will be rebuilt, the nations will flock to Jerusalem (Is. 2:2-3), and the converted Israel will be the focal point of world events. And so the return of the Jewish people to Palestine is a sign of the imminence of the first return of Christ and the thousand-year reign.

This is the basic outline of the thousand-year reign as it is commonly viewed. Details may differ. Hal Lindsey, for example, sees the first return of Christ in terms of the Rapture, when the believers suddenly disappear to form the Church in heaven during the next seven years of the Tribulation on earth. In Lindsey's view, the second return of Christ will usher in the thousand-year reign, at the end of which will come the destruction of the present world, the final judgment, and the completion of all things.

In this representation, the Church of the New Testament functions only as an interlude within the drama of God's plan. In the first act, God made a covenant with His people Israel, that is, the Jews. When they rejected the Messiah, the curtain was drawn. For the interlude God goes into the byways to gather the Church from among the Gentiles. But soon the second and final act will begin: Israel will get a second chance. During the thousand-year reign, it will again live in the promised land, and then eventually will be converted. This will be the fulfillment of the Old Testament and the climax of God's historical drama.

It's as if there were a twofold Christ. There is the Christ of the New Testament Church, and then there is the Jewish Messiah, who will return shortly. It is not by chance that Lindsey constantly speaks of "the Jewish Messiah."

To represent the New Testament Church as nothing but an interlude is clearly in conflict with Scripture, which portrays the New Testament not as a detour but as the direct continuation and fulfillment of the old covenant. The Old Testament laws concerning foods and feasts were "only a shadow of what is to come; but the substance belongs to Christ" (Col. 2:17). The priests of the old covenant only serve as "a copy and shadow of the heavenly sanctuary" (Heb. 8:5). Christ is the High Priest of the new covenant about which Jeremiah prophesied (Jer. 31) and which has now been made with us. This High Priest carries out His function in the sanctuary, in the true tabernacle in heaven (Heb. 8:1-2).

The whole Old Testament has become reality in Christ. The New Testament paints this fact in various colors, Christ is the true expiation (Rom. 3:25), the true circumcision (Col. 2:11), the true paschal lamb (I Cor. 5:7), and the true offering (Eph. 5:2). Therefore the Church of this Christ, gathered in the New Testament era, can be no interlude but must be the fulfillment of the Old Testament.

A careful study of the New Testament makes this even clearer. Christ's body, the Church, is the true seed of Abraham, the true Israel, and the true people of God (Matt. 1:21; Luke 1:17; Rom. 9:25-6; II Cor. 6:16-18; Gal. 3:29; Titus 2.14; Heb. 8:8-10; James 1:1, 18; I Pet. 2:9; Rev. 21:3, 12). She is also the true temple of God (I Cor. 3:16; II Cor. 6:16; Eph. 2:22; II Thess. 2:4; Heb. 8:2). The Church is further described as Zion and as the true Jerusalem (Gal. 4:26; Heb. 12:22; Rev. 3:12; 21:2, 10).

Neither the New Testament nor the Church is an interlude. Rather, it was the covenant with Israel that was temporary. That covenant was meant to disappear and be recast as the new covenant of Jeremiah 31. The Letter to the Hebrews, in quoting Jeremiah 31 makes clear that the prophecy about this new covenant pertains to the believers in Christ, who now fulfill the prophecy.

The old and new covenants form an essential unity which we may not break. The new covenant is the continuation and fulfillment of the old, and the Church is the continuation of the Old Testament people of God. From the beginning God had planned that the Gentiles would also share in salvation; in Genesis 12:3 He says to Abraham: "By you all the families of the earth shall bless themselves."

And so Paul often points back to Abraham, the father of all believers, both circumcised and uncircumcised (Rom. 4:11). He also says: "In Christ Jesus the blessing of Abraham might come upon the Gentiles, that we might receive the promise of the Spirit through faith" (Gal. 3:14 RSV). It becomes crystal clear who Abraham's seed is in the apostolic statement: "And if you are Christ's, then you are Abraham's offspring, heirs according to promise" (vs. 29 RSV).

This is the "mystery of Christ," that the believers from among the Gentiles are now fellow citizens with the saints and members of the household of God, built upon the same foundation of the apostles and prophets (Eph. 2:19-20). The mystery of Christ "was not made known to the sons of men in other generations as it has now been revealed to his holy apostles and prophets by the Spirit; that is, how the Gentiles are fellow heirs, members of the same body, and partakers of the promise in Christ Jesus through the gospel" (Eph. 3:5-6 RSV). This does not mean that people earlier had been totally ignorant of this "mystery." Although God did reveal Christ's redemptive work and the participation of the Gentiles in it in the Old Testament, He did not do so to the same extent as He has now done through the Holy Spirit. The details of the mystery of Christ have now been proclaimed far and wide.

The calling of the Gentiles is therefore not something surprisingly new; it is simply the putting into effect of the eternal plan of God, which He did not fully reveal until Christ was crucified on Golgotha. It was then that the curtain of the temple was torn in two, because the true High Priest had made His sacrifice whereby the dividing wall of hostility between Jews and Gentiles was broken down (Eph. 2:14ff). That was God's plan from the beginning. Even the prophets were aware of the future participation of the Gentiles in God's salvation, for Peter writes to the New Testament church that the prophets "prophesied of the grace that was to be yours" (I Pet. 1:10).

The covenant with the nation of Israel, which no longer exists, was made on Mount Horeb (Ex. 19:3-6). Jeremiah proclaimed that it would eventually disappear, and it did finally end with the devastation of Jerusalem in A.D. 70. Israel's privilege of being a holy nation and God's own people was passed on to the believers in Christ among the Gentiles (I Pet. 2:9-10). The Church has now replaced the nation of Israel in all respects. The temple to which the sacrifices were brought has disappeared, since Christ has brought His sacrifice. The theocracy of Israel and the throne of David in Jerusalem have disappeared forever, because Christ's throne is now in heaven. Christ told the Sanhedrin that the prophecy of Psalm 110 would be fulfilled in Himself: He would be seated at the right hand of God, on His throne (Matt. 26:64). Christ is the Priest-King of Psalm 110, who ascends His throne by way of His priestly sacrifice.

Israel's time has passed. A Kingdom of peace is coming to the earth, but only after the resurrection of the last day, when the New Jerusalem will descend out of heaven and all people will dwell in God's tent (Rev. 21:3).

A Conversion of Israel in the End Times?

But, we may ask, isn't the promise of salvation made

to the nation of Israel? Doesn't Paul state this when he reveals a "mystery," namely, that a hardening has come upon part of Israel until the full number of Gentiles come in, so all Israel will be saved? (Rom. 11:25-6).

It is not correct to say that Paul's words apply to the would-be end times, in which a conversion of the Jews will take place. There is no suggestion here of the conver- *Correct* sion of the whole Jewish nation. Rather, in Romans 11 Paul is dealing with what is happening in his time.

In Romans 11 he begins with a question: "Has God rejected His people?" The answer is "By no means!" The proof is Paul himself: "I myself am an Israelite, a descendant of Abraham, a member of the tribe of Benjamin." Later in the same chapter Paul talks about his own calling: "Inasmuch then as I am an apostle to the Gentiles, I magnify my ministry in order to make my fellow Jews jealous, and thus save some of them" (Rom. 11:13-14 RSV). In these passages Paul is concerned not with a distant future but with what is happening in his time.

God does not exclusively call the Gentiles to salvation after the rejection of Christ by Israel. Previously God's call had been an exclusive matter—only Israel, not the Gentiles. But now God calls both Gentiles and Jews. Paul is witness to the conversion of the Gentiles in his day; God graciously uses this conversion to call again upon His people, the Jews. "Some of them" (Rom. 11:14) ✳ C will become jealous of the Gentiles and so come to faith. In this way, the reaction to the conversion of the Gentiles will bring about the salvation of "all Israel."

"All Israel" does not refer to all Jews but to the believing remnant that repents and believes in Jesus ✳ C Christ. The prophecy about the new covenant (Jer. 31) in which God takes away sins applies also to the converted Jews (Rom. 11:27). The new covenant does not differ essentially from the old covenant, in which the promises

were made on the condition of faith and obedience:
"Now therefore, if you will obey my voice and keep my
covenant, you shall be my own possession among all
peoples" (Ex. 19:5 RSV). The time in which Paul
preached was still a time of grace for Israel. The Jews
could keep God's covenant by listening to the gospel of
Christ and accepting that the covenant was fulfilled in
Christ; then they, along with the Gentiles, would belong
to God's own people.

No, Paul is not referring to an Israel of the end times.
When he speaks of "all Israel," he is not speaking of the
nation of Israel as we know it today. For that matter, it
would not be a very great miracle if the Israel of the end
times were saved, since that would include only a fraction of the race of Israel; it would mean that millions of
Jews who were dead by then would be lost.

Paul is speaking about the time in which he lived.
"Just as you were once disobedient to God but now have
received mercy because of their disobedience, so they have
now been disobedient in order that by the mercy shown
to you they also may now[1] receive mercy" (Rom. 11:30-1
RSV). The "now" refers to what is going on in Paul's
time, when Israel had not been definitively rejected as
God's people. It is an interim period, a day when grace is
still available to Israel.[2] Their "acceptance" remained a

---

1. The *Oxford Annotated Revised Standard Version*, although it
omits the word *now*, states in a footnote that other ancient authorities
include it.—TRANS.

2. J. van Bruggen observes that the first preaching of the gospel in
Rome had not led to a decisive stage in the confrontation with the
synagogue. The Jews in Rome knew much about Christianity (Acts
28:22), and still wished to listen to the gospel (vs. 23). The division was
not fully completed until after Paul's preaching (vs. 24ff). Only then
does Paul excommunicate the Jews in the name of the Holy Spirit (*Het
Raadsel van Romeinen 16* (Groningen, 1970), pp. 34-5).

possibility, and Paul hoped for it and worked for it. It
will be a great miracle: they will pass from death to life.[3]
But when that time of grace has passed and Jerusalem has
been destroyed, Israel as a nation will no longer be God's
people. We today can no longer say that the Jews are
"beloved for the sake of their forefathers" (Rom. 11:28).
Israel no longer has special privileges; her particular role
in the history of redemption has ended.

Revelation 20:1-10

But doesn't Revelation 20 tell us about a thousand-
year reign?

We have noted that some people see the thousand-
year reign as a period of exactly 1,000 years, in which
Christ rules on David's throne in Jerusalem. Israel, which
has been converted and has returned to Palestine, rules
with Christ over a world that enjoys unparalleled
prosperity. Then satan is unbound; in his last assault he
gathers the nations against Israel. But Christ comes to
judge.

Hal Lindsey's own variation on this theme is that the

Van Bruggen writes: "Whoever reads Paul's views on the status of
the Jews and the future of Israel must ask himself to what extent these
views stem from the unique situation of the church of Rome at the time
when the apostle is writing his letter" (p. 35).

3. If one takes the acceptance of Israel to be an event of the end
times, then "from death to life" would refer to the resurrection at the
last day, or an event directly related to it. But the concern of the
passage here is not with the effect of Israel's acceptance on the world,
but on Israel itself. That the Israelites who have rejected the Messiah
come to accept Him and are received by God will be an inexplicable
wonder. Then they will rise from death and come to life.

thousand-year reign will not begin until the battle of Armageddon has been fought and Christ has returned to the Mount of Olives, from where He had ascended into heaven. At the end of the reign, some of the children of the believers will begin a rebellion against Christ and His rule. "Christ will bring swift judgment upon them before the rebellion reaches the actual fighting stage" (PE, 166; see Rev. 20:7-10). After that He will create a new universe.

Obviously Lindsey does not know what to do with the setting free of satan because in his scheme the conflict between Gog and Magog has already taken place during the Battle of Armageddon. Therefore he speaks of "some of the children of the believers," who start a rebellion. Then he goes on to speak of the suppression of that rebellion, which occurs without resort to violence. This is a strange reading of Revelation 20:7ff, which says that satan will be loosed to deceive the nations and gather them together for battle against the Church. Lindsey needs to scale down the conflict so that his scheme will not fall apart.

Revelation 20 tells us that satan will be bound for a certain period ("one thousand years"), and then will be set free "for a little while" (vs. 3), whereupon he will deceive the nations and gather them for war (vs. 7ff). Finally the devil will be thrown into the lake of fire, and the last judgment will take place.

A crucial question is whether these "one thousand years" indicate a period of time in the future, or one that has already begun. To answer it, we must decide whether the events of Revelation 20 follow chronologically upon the events of Revelation 19. In chapter 20 the history of the world has already come to an end: Babylon has fallen, the marriage supper of the Lamb has been celebrated, Christ has appeared, the last battle has been fought, and the beast and the false prophet have been thrown into the lake of fire. According to verse 14, the lake of fire is not opened until after the final judgment. And so we see that chapter 19 arrives at the same ending of the world that is described in chapter 20:10-15. There is no time left for a thousand-year reign. ✱ NOTE

Therefore Revelation 20 cannot be a chronological continuation of Revelation 19. This means that we here encounter the same phenomenon we have seen several times in the book of Revelation: events that are described consecutively in reality take place at the same time. The seven seals, the seven trumpets, and the seven bowls did not follow each other chronologically but ran parallel to each other and brought us time and again to the end of world history. Similarly, the events of chapter 20 run parallel to the events described in earlier chapters.

In the beginning of chapter 20, John sees an angel come down from heaven with the key of the bottomless pit and a great chain. The angel seizes satan and binds him for one thousand years. This passage is very similar to Revelation 12:7ff, where Michael and his angels fought with the dragon, conquered him, and threw him out of heaven to the earth. This occurred when Christ ascended (see Rev. 12:5). Two other passages of Scripture (Matt. 12:29 and Col. 2:15), show us that Christ conquered satan through His death on the cross. The ascension occurred soon after the crucifixion, and Christ ascended the throne in heaven on the grounds of His sacrifice on Golgotha. On the basis of the above we can conclude that the "one thousand years" began when Christ conquered satan on the cross and ascended into heaven. The "one thousand years" will end with the last events of world history: the setting free of satan, the sentencing of satan, and the final judging of the world. Therefore the "one thousand years" embrace the whole period from the crucifixion and ascension to a short time before Christ's return.

This is to say that we view the number "one thousand" symbolically. It was never meant to indicate a rule of Christ lasting exactly ten centuries. This image of one thousand years is a symbol, as are many other images in the book of Revelation. (If you're going to read the text literally, you must be consistent. This would involve believing that satan is actually lying somewhere bound to a very long chain.) One thousand (10 x 10 x 10), as the number of completion, indicates that Christ completes the task that He has begun. While he is bound, satan is Christ's prisoner. His temporary prison is "the abyss" (Luke 8:31). From there he will be freed, and then he will be subjected to the eternal torture of the lake of fire.

The imprisoned satan does enjoy a certain limited freedom of activity. He is limited in that he can "deceive the nations no more" (Rev. 20:3). From the time of the ascension to the time of Christ's return, satan is not allowed to prevent the preaching of the gospel. Satan must retreat while the gospel advances across the globe.

In the first three verses of chapter 20, the binding of satan elucidates the history of the Church of the New Testament. We must also let the binding of satan elucidate verses 4-6, where John sees thrones, and the souls of those who were beheaded for their testimony to Jesus and for the Word of God. They came to life and reigned with Christ for a thousand years. This is the first resurrection, we are told.

Is there a hint here of a bodily resurrection? No, it was the *souls* of the martyrs that John saw. They were sitting on thrones reminiscent of the thrones placed around the "Ancient of Days" in Daniel 7. That is where the "souls" are now, and they are privileged to reign with Christ.

In verse 4, the Revised Standard Version incorrectly reads: "And they came to life and reigned with Christ." It should read: "And they lived, and reigned with Christ."[5] Their souls are taken up into heaven immediately following the death of their bodies (Rev. 14:13). They are seated upon the thrones, one by one, as they come in out of the heat of persecution.

Christ pointed to this first resurrection when He said: "He who believes in me, though he die, yet shall he live." (John 11:25 RSV). Already in the days of John there were some whose bodies were resurrected before the thousand-year reign. But they did not take part in the first resurrection, which refers to the living and ruling with Christ of those who have died during the thousand years, and they will continue to do so after that period of time has ended. This continuation is indicated in verse 6: "Blessed and holy is he who shares in the first resurrection! Over such the second death has no power." The second death is the lake of fire (vs. 14). But if there is a second death, there is also a second resurrection. This second resurrection is indirectly indicated by the fact that a *first* resurrection must precede another one.

John writes that the rest of the dead did not live until the thousand years were ended. This does not mean that they lived afterwards, for when they died, they entered the eternal death. They will be raised up during the final judgment, but they won't become alive in the true sense

---

5. The Greek for "they lived" and "they reigned" is the same.

of the word. Instead, thrown into the lake of fire (Rev. 20:15), they will sink even deeper into death. Because they did not participate in the first resurrection, they will remain dead during the thousand years and thereafter in eternity. That these dead did not live until the thousand years were ended simply tells us what went on *during* that period.

Is there a suggestion here of a special *kingdom*, such as is alluded to in the expression "thousand year reign" or "millennial kingdom"? There is none at all; indeed, there is no room for an earthly theocracy after the ascension and Pentecost. Neither is there a suggestion of a bodily resurrection. Revelation 20 informs us not about what happens on earth but about what happens behind the clouds, in the world of the dead.

Revelation 20 concerns itself with the same period of time as the preceding chapters. From them we learned how the Church here below, beneath the clouds, was oppressed. But in chapter 20 we are allowed to peek behind the curtains to see that those who were beheaded are seated on thrones and reign immediately. "Here below we see the drama unfolding—unburied corpses that are kicked around. Up above is the real theater, where these same people sit on thrones and judge the world."[6] In this chapter we view the history of the Church, its struggle, its persecution, and its martyrdom, in the light of the victory of Christ. However much satan raves and rages, Christ maintains His rule.

The next few verses (20:7-10) must also be read in

6. Klaas Schilder, *De Openbaring van Johannes en het sociale leven*, p. 264.

the light of Christ's victory. From them we learn that satan will be released when the thousand years come to an end, when they reach their peak. But this new freedom of satan's will pose no real threat to God's work. This episode is actually a comfort to us: the fact that satan's release soon ends with his final and permanent judgment consoles us, for it tells us that the first resurrection is unassailable even in the face of satan's last effort to overturn God's work.

But how do we understand the Biblical message about the release of satan? We are told that he will come out to deceive the nations at the four corners of the earth, that is, Gog and Magog, to gather them for war. Does this mean that there will be a war complete with marching armies, tanks, and cannons? Will satan really mobilize all the nations in a final war? Who are these nations at the four corners of the earth? Are they, as people sometimes say, the most distant nations, the savage, uncultivated barbarians, for example, the armies of Africa and China? Where will they assemble? We read: "And they marched up over the broad earth and surrounded the camp of the saints and the beloved city" (20:9 RSV). The expression "the camp of the saints" reminds us of the Israelite camp in the desert, and "the beloved city" of course makes us think of the city of Jerusalem.

These expressions are of no great help in deciding where the nations will gather, since they function as symbolic references to the Church of the New Testament. Is the Church a specific place? Is it Europe, the Netherlands, or even the United States? We today, at least, are no longer tempted to make such identifications. But when the hordes arrive, where will they come from, and what will they surround?

We will never get anywhere if we look at the line of

demarcation between satan's armies and God's people in geographical terms. We must also drop the idea of a war fought with conventional weapons. These verses simply do not refer to nations that are literally to be found on the map, nor to a war that is to be fought with literal armies.

This becomes evident when we compare this prophecy to the parallel prophecy in Ezekiel 38. Ezekiel speaks of Gog, of the land of Magog, who as chief prince of Meshech and Tubal marshals the nations against Israel. This struggle is placed within a definite historical framework. But in Revelation 20, the concrete details fade away. The enemy now approaches "from the four corners of the earth," and "Gog of the land of Magog" becomes "Gog and Magog." This indicates that historical details are no longer important.

Other concerns come to the fore here. Satan is involved with his typical work of deception: he deceives the nations to assemble them for war against Israel. But this is no war of tanks and cannons; it is a war of spiritual infiltration. As the Scriptures tell us, "We are not contending against flesh and blood, but against the principalities, against the powers, against the world rulers of this present darkness, against the spiritual hosts of wickedness in the heavenly places" (Eph. 6:12 RSV). This spiritual infiltration prevails everywhere, in China as well as in America, in Africa as well as in the Netherlands. The antithesis cannot be sketched on a world map, for God makes His move on the basis of another kind of map.

Some people imagine that during the end times, savage armies under satan's leadership will swoop down on the "civilized" and supposedly Christian Western world. It is more correct and more helpful to perceive the enemy as the infiltration of evil that deceives people everywhere around us.

The question remains as to whether we today are

living during the time of satan's release. All we can say is that there are many indications that satan is now free. However, we are not permitted to engage in calculation and speculation. Only when Christ returns will we learn how long satan was free, and whether we lived during the "little while" of satan's release. We must also realize that the "little while" cannot be viewed according to our notions of time: it could be a year or many centuries.

A time is coming, say the Scriptures, when the gospel will be in retreat and satan will be free. But Christ will still be in control during that time. Satan's deceptions will not confound God's work. God will show that He is the King of heaven when He sends fire to the earth to consume the masses who followed satan, and when He casts the great deceiver into the lake of fire.

5

A Seven-Year Countdown?

Some time in the future there will be a seven-year period climaxed by the visible return of Jesus Christ.

Most prophecies which have not yet been fulfilled concern events which will develop shortly before the beginning of and during this seven-year countdown.

The general time of this seven-year period couldn't begin until the Jewish people re-established their nation in their ancient homeland of Palestine (PE, 32).

The big question for us will be whether the Scriptures disclose such a period of seven years as Lindsey has outlined above.

Lindsey's notion of a seven-year period has its source in Revelation 11:2-3:

> But do not measure the court outside the temple; leave that out, for it is given over to the nations, and they will trample over the holy city for forty-two months. And I will grant my two witnesses power to prophesy for one thousand two hundred and sixty days, clothed in sackcloth.

70

But how does Lindsey arrive at a period of seven years? He explains this a little further on:

> This seven-year period we have called the "count-down" is a period of unique events. There is more prophecy concerning this period than any other era the Bible describes.
>
> The apostle John counted out seven years for this period when he spoke of the second half being forty-two months (i.e. 3 1/2 years), and the first half being 1260 days (i.e., 3 1/2 x 360 days, which is the Biblical year) (Revelation 11:2,3) (PE, 33-4).

The reader will have noticed that Lindsey adds the two periods of 3 1/2 years together to arrive at seven years. Revelation 11 mentions first that the nations will trample the holy city for 42 months. This Lindsey calls "the second half" of the seven years. The passage then tells us about the prophecy of the 1260 days by the two witnesses. This second reference to 3 1/2 years Lindsey terms "the first half" of the seven-year period.

Why does he do this? Lindsey's interpretation of Revelation 11 is closely connected with his explanation of the "seventy weeks" of Daniel 9:24: "Seventy weeks of years are decreed concerning your people and your holy city . . ." (RSV). Lindsey says a week of years is seven years, and therefore the period indicated lasts 70 x 7 years, or 490 years.

Then Lindsey gets out his calculator. He figures out that the time when the Jews were granted permission to return to Jerusalem and rebuild the city and the temple to the time of the coming of the Messiah was 483 years, or 69 weeks of years. The last "week" of seven years is therefore still missing. That period, in which God will definitely establish His Kingdom, has been postponed to the final phase of world history. In the interim the Christian

Church is being gathered. But at the end of history God will
again turn to Israel. That will happen during the seven
years of the Tribulation, which, according to Daniel
9:27, is split into two parts: during half the week,
sacrifice and offering cease.

And so Christ's coming or advent is supposed to last
seven years! Everything that Revelation describes as the
unfolding plan of God (ch. 6-19) is to take place during
the seven years when the believers will be in heaven and
Israel plays a central role in world politics.

With the help of the prophecies and the book of
Revelation, Lindsey sets about describing the events of
the seven-year advent in careful detail. For him prophecy
is like a reel of film which, when played backwards, is
more timely than tomorrow morning's newspaper. His
conception of Revelation is clearly determined by three
things: his view that Revelation bears on an "end time" of
seven years, his view of Israel, and his view that the
prophets must be interpreted "literally," all of which we
have already discussed.

Can Lindsey justify his notion of a seven-year advent
or countdown on the basis of Scripture? Right now we
will make several observations about Revelation 11; we
will defer the discussion of Daniel 9 to Chapter 11.

Revelation 11 begins with a message of comfort for
the oppressed church. It is important to note in what way
the church was being oppressed. The sixth trumpet
revealed that mankind did not repent of its murders, sor-
ceries, immorality, or theft. This unrepentant attitude of
the unbelievers causes great stress to the true believers. In
the midst of this, God sends His message of comfort: He
says to John: "Rise and measure the temple of God and

the altar and those who worship there" (Rev. 11:1 RSV). His job was to delimit the temple in order to safeguard it against danger.

What is meant by "the temple of God"? Could it mean the temple of stone in Jerusalem? Not likely, since that temple was not secured against attack in A.D. 70; rather, it was "trampled" or completely destroyed. Besides, Christ said to the Jews, "Behold, your house is forsaken" (Matt. 23:38; Luke 13:35). In other words, the temple was no longer God's house.

We must look elsewhere for the meaning of "the temple of God." Several passages from the New Testament (I Cor. 3:16-17; II Cor. 6:16; Eph. 2:21) inform us that the true temple now is the body of Christ, that is, the believers in Christ.

When Revelation 11 speaks about "the altar," we must think of any place from where prayers are sent up to heaven. Mention is also made of those who worship in the temple. These are the true believers whom God will protect. The hostile powers are not able to trample them into the ground. That is not to say that they won't experience severe persecution. In fact, Revelation 11 tells us that the beast from out of the abyss will put them to death. But the pagan power won't subjugate them permanently, because the Lord has His eternal Kingdom waiting for them. They shall be more than conquerors!

John was not to measure the court around the outside of the temple, because God had rejected it. The outer court represents those who are found within the church but, in God's book, are not part of it. They are not true believers: their faith and piety are mere show. They will be destroyed, since the outer court has been given to the nations, who will trample the holy city for 42 months.

That the nations will trample the holy city may remind us of Jesus' words: "Jerusalem will be trodden down by the Gentiles" (Luke 21:24). However, Revelation 11:2 does not refer to the destruction of Jerusalem in A.D. 70.[1] Something else is intended here. This becomes clear when we pay attention to the period of time (42 months) during which the holy city will be ravaged.

Lindsey says that these 42 months are the second half of the seven-year countdown, and that this will take place during the very last stage of world history. But a careful reading of Revelation tells us something completely different about the beginning and the end of this period. The first thing we must realize is that the 42 months refer to the same period as the 1260 days of Revelation.

In order to determine when this period begins, we should look at Revelation 12:6: "And the woman fled into the wilderness, where she has a place prepared by God, in which to be nourished for one thousand two hundred and sixty days." This occurs after the woman has borne her son, who is caught up to God and His throne (Rev. 12:5). Because this verse refers to Christ's birth and ascension, the subsequent period of 1260 days or 42 months must begin with Christ's ascension.

But when does the period end? Revelation 11 again draws us to the end of history. The two witnesses have completed their testimony, the second woe has passed,

---

1. The phrase "the holy city" in the Old Testament refers to Jerusalem (Ps. 24:3; Is. 48:2). It was "holy" because Yahweh lived there in His temple and was worshiped there. Jerusalem was still called "the holy city" at the beginning of Christ's public ministry (Matt. 4:5). But the temple had ceased to be "the house of God" when the Jews took Jesus outside the city gate to crucify Him. The tearing of the curtain of the temple from top to bottom signaled this change (Matt. 27:51). From that moment God departed from the temple, and Christ's words were fulfilled: "Behold, your house is forsaken and desolate" (Matt. 23:38). Jerusalem then ceased to be "the holy city."

and the third woe follows it immediately, at the same time that the seventh angel blows the trumpet (Rev. 11:15).

Therefore the period of 42 months or 1260 days embraces the whole New Testament era from Christ's ascension to His return. During that period the two witnesses, the true evangelists, proclaim the Word of God in a prophetic manner throughout the world.

However, obstacles are placed in their path by the "nations" who trample the holy city during the 42 months, during the New Testament era. Therefore the time of the proclamation of the Word is simultaneously a time of church persecution and dissolution.

But still the witness of the gospel prevails, and through it the Lord continues to gather His Church. God sustains the true Church, the true worship of His name, and the true worshipers; He protects them from the violence of the Antichrist. The beast out of the abyss may persecute the witnessing Church for 42 months, but the Lord will give the final victory to His witnesses!

6

Matthew 24: Jesus' Prophetic Address to His Disciples

"Jesus the Prophet"

Lindsey uses the subtitle "Jesus the Prophet" for his discussion of the Savior's teachings in Matthew 24 and parallel passages. Near the beginning of the chapter, the disciples had asked, "Tell us, when will this be, and what will be the sign of your coming and of the close of the age?" Lindsey treats the chapter in terms of the events that will precede Christ's return. He makes a serious mistake when he ignores the first part of the question: "When will this be?"

Careful study of the text will show that "this" refers to the destruction of the temple in Jerusalem. Christ had just spoken about that event in Matthew 23:38: "Behold, your house is forsaken and desolate." Shortly thereafter the disciples point out to Jesus the beautiful buildings of the temple. Jesus says, "You see all these, do you not? Truly, I say to you, there will not be left here one stone upon another, that will not be thrown down." It is this statement that leads the disciples to ask: "Tell us, when will this be? When will the destruction of Jerusalem and the temple occur?"

Because Lindsey ignores this question and its context, he is able to read a lot of things into the text that are simply not there. This allows him to say that at the time of Christ's return, the Jews will be living in Palestine. After all, doesn't Jesus say that those who are *in Judea* should flee to the mountains (in order to survive the battles that will precede Jesus' return)? On the strength of Christ's command "Pray that your flight may not be . . . on a sabbath," Lindsey claims that the sabbath will again be kept in the land of the Jews before the return of Christ.

"When will this be?"

We should not be misled by the heading "Signs of the End" found above Matthew 24 in many Bibles. In actual fact, the chapter is concerned with the destruction of Jerusalem and the events that will precede it. It is true that later in the chapter (vs. 29-31), Christ does proclaim the coming end of the world; He does this in connection with the approaching downfall of Jerusalem.

Christ warns His disciples, in the context of Jerusalem's destruction, to "take heed that no one leads you astray" (vs. 4). Dreadful things such as wars, famines and earthquakes will happen. But these will still not indicate the end (of Jerusalem). First nation will rise against nation and kingdom against kingdom.[1] That is an ac-

---

1. A similar statement is found in two places in the Old Testament; in both places it refers to the disintegration of a kingdom. In II Chronicles 15:6 we read, "They were broken in pieces, nation against nation and city against city, for God troubled them with every sort of distress." These words of the prophet Azariah referred to the distress at

curate picture of the Jewish nation in A.D. 66-70. Not only were the Jews at war with the Romans, there was also conflict between all sorts of splinter groups and little kingdoms, each with its own leader who pretended to be the Christ, the anointed King of Israel.

Something else would happen before this conflict would break out into a civil war. Luke 21:12 tells us that the events would take place in a definite chronological order: "But before all this they will lay their hands on you and persecute you, delivering you up to the synagogues and prisons, and you will be brought before kings and governors for my name's sake." The disciples will suffer persecution on account of their proclamation of the gospel of Jesus Christ. In Mark 13:9 Christ tells the disciples: "But take heed to yourselves; for they will deliver you up to councils; and you will be beaten in synagogues; and you will stand before governors and kings for my sake, to bear testimony before them."

All this indeed happened. The book of Acts is the story of the persecution of the apostles, their trials before councils, and their testimonies before Jewish judges and Gentile governors.[2] These things continued for another five years or so after the end of the book of Acts. Paul came to Rome in about A.D. 61 (Acts 28:16); in A.D. 66, the disturbances preceding the destruction of Jerusalem began.

The first part of Matthew 24 deals with the time of Acts. When Christ says, "And this gospel of the kingdom will be preached throughout the whole world, as a

---

the time of the judges. In Isaiah 19:2, "city against city, kingdom against kingdom" refers to events in Egypt. Therefore Christ in Matthew 24:7 was proclaiming the disintegration of the Jewish nation. Israel would be judged for having rejected her King.

2. See Acts 4:1ff; 5:17ff; 6:12ff; 7:54ff; 12:1-3; 13:50ff; 14:19; 17:13; 18:12ff; 21:27ff.

testimony to all nations; and then the end will come" (vs. 14), "the end" refers to the destruction of Jerusalem. In the parallel passage in Mark's gospel, the same word is used for "testimony" (13:9) as in this verse from Matthew. Mark is clearly referring to the preaching of the gospel by the disciples before the destruction of Jerusalem.

"Throughout the whole *world*" does not mean the world that will exist at the time of Christ's return. The Greek reads, "in the *oikoumené,*" which at that time referred to the area surrounding the Mediterranean Sea, the known world of that time. If Paul carried out his intention to visit Spain (see Rom. 15:24), we can say that by A.D. 66, the gospel of the Kingdom had been preached to the whole world, to the *oikoumené*, the known world of that time.

We must be very clear that the reference to the preaching of the gospel in Matthew relates exclusively to the period preceding the destruction of Jerusalem. We do not thereby wish to cast doubt on the Church's mission task. Not at all! That task originates in the command to the Church to proclaim the gospel to the world (Matt. 28:19). We simply need to distinguish the task of the apostles from the task of the church of the ages, which is to carry on the apostolic witness to the world.

In this way we will avoid the calculation of the time of Christ's return. We will not be tempted to determine the present extent of the preaching of the gospel in the world so as to figure out how soon Christ will return. We are not allowed to make such calculations. The Kingdom of God simply does not come in such a way that we can calculate its arrival, Christ tells us (Luke 17:20-1).

The Sign of His Coming

The disciples had not only asked Jesus, "When will this be?" (namely, the destruction of Jerusalem), but also, "What will be the sign of Your coming?" What did the disciples mean by Jesus' *coming*? Were they referring to His return? Or were they thinking of another appearance of Jesus?

Notice that the expression "the coming of the Son of man" occurs in Matthew 24:27: "For as the lightning comes from the east and shines as far as the west, so will be the coming of the Son of man." This next section of Matthew 24, verses 15-28, is therefore probably the part of Jesus' speech that answers the disciples' question about the sign of His coming. The disciples must have been thinking of the glorious appearance of Christ at the time of the judgment of Jerusalem.

When the Bible speaks about a "coming" of the Lord Jesus, we immediately think of His return. But here Christ spoke to the disciples about the coming of the Son of man in a more immediate context. Matthew 10:23 helps to make this clear: "When they persecute you in one town, flee to the next; for truly, I say to you, you will not have gone through all the towns of Israel, before the Son of man comes." In other words, Christ says that the Son of man will "come" even before the disciples will have traveled in missionary capacity to all the towns of Israel.

We must understand "the towns of Israel" to mean all towns where a Jewish community was found, therefore also the cities in countries outside of Palestine. Jesus elsewhere says to His disciples: "Beware of men; for they will deliver you up to councils, and flog you in their synagogues, and you will be dragged before governors and kings for my sake, to bear testimony before them and the Gentiles" (Matt. 10:17-18 RSV). These words describe the situation that is familiar to us from the book of Acts. They speak of the period in which the gospel is preached first to the Jew and then to the Gentile.

That was a relatively short period. We may assume that many of the disciples were no longer living at the time of Jerusalem's destruction in A.D. 70. They had not even reached all the cities of Israel with the gospel. The destruction of Jerusalem ended Israel's position of priority. That was the "coming" of the Son of man!

The end of Matthew 23 speaks of the "coming" of Christ in a similar manner: "Behold, your house is forsaken and desolate. For I tell you, you will not see me again, until you say, 'Blessed is he who comes in the name of the Lord.' " Christ here announces to Jerusalem its coming judgment. That their house is forsaken means that the glory of the Lord will depart from the temple. Israel will be stuck with an empty temple. Jesus will leave them. But at a certain time He will return, and then they will greet Him as King, using the words of Psalm 118:26: "Blessed be he who enters in the name of the Lord!"

The Jews had greeted Jesus with these words when He made His triumphal entry into Jerusalem (see Luke 19:38). At a certain time He was to return as King, at which time they would again say, "Blessed be he who enters in the name of the Lord!" But it will be too late; it will only be a forced recognition of the kingship of Christ, whom they have rejected. This will take place when Christ comes in glory to execute the sentence against the apostate—at one time religious—city of Jerusalem.

Jesus' reference to this event is the occasion for the disciples' question about the sign of His coming, which will take place at the time of Jerusalem's judgment. But how do we know that the downfall of Jerusalem was at hand? That becomes clear in verses 15-28.

"So when you see the desolating sacrilege spoken of

by the prophet Daniel, standing in the holy place (let the reader understand) . . . ." The desolating sacrilege or abomination in the holy place is the sign of the coming of Christ. It indicates to the disciples that the destruction of Jerusalem and the temple are at hand. The disciples understood this language; in terms of Scripture, sacrilege involves the use of idols. "Desolating sacrilege" refers to the idolatrous worship that desolates the service of the Lord.

The Savior refers to the prophecy of Daniel. Let the reader understand! There are various references to "the desolating sacrilege" in Daniel. An example is Daniel 9:27. (In the RSV, "abomination" is used for "sacrilege.")

> And he shall make a strong covenant with many for one week; and for half of the week he shall cause sacrifice and offering to cease; and upon the wing of abominations shall come one who makes desolate, until the decreed end is poured out on the desolator.

This is an allusion to Antiochus Epiphanes, the Syrian king, who during his reign from 175-164 B.C. persecuted the Jews severely. He prohibited sacrifice and offering; the Jews were no longer allowed to bring their offerings to the Lord in the temple in Jerusalem. Antiochus placed an image of Zeus, the king of the Greek gods, upon the altar of the Lord. Swine, unclean beasts, were offered on the altar. This was the desolating abomination in the holy place (Dan. 11:31; 12:11). When Christ says, "Let the reader understand," He means that this desolating sacrilege is going to happen once again in the holy place. In the Jewish war with the Romans, the temple will in one way or another again be desecrated. That will be the sign of the imminence of the fall of Jerusalem and the majestic appearance of Christ as judge. With an eye to that time, Christ commands, "Let those who are in Judea flee to the mountains."

It is now easy to understand that these words give no indication (as Lindsey claims) that the Jews will be living in Palestine as a nation at the time of Christ's return. Christ was speaking of A.D. 70, when Jerusalem was destroyed. The disciples who were still alive at that time, and the Christians in Jerusalem, obeyed Jesus' command: they fled from the city, taking refuge near Pella, which lies southeast of the Lake of Gennesaret.

It is now also easy to understand that Christ's words, "Pray that your flight may not be on a sabbath," cannot be used to argue that the sabbath will again be kept in a future, reborn Jewish state. But what about Christ's words in verse 21: "For then there will be great tribulation, such as has not been from the beginning of the world until now, no, and never will be"? Don't they refer to a still-to-come end of the world?

Let's not be misled, by what usually comes to mind when we hear such words. We must read these words, too, in relation to the flight from Jerusalem in A.D. 70. Christ tells the disciples that they must flee to the mountains when they see the downfall of Jerusalem approaching. They must also pray that their flight will be neither in winter nor on the sabbath, "for then there will be great tribulation . . . ." "Then" refers to the time immediately preceding Jerusalem's destruction.

Yes, someone may argue, but it does say that the great tribulation will be "such as has not been from the beginning of the world until now, no, and never will be." Surely this refers to the end of the world!

The question is understandable. But if we compare Scripture with Scripture, it will become clear that Matthew 24:21 does not necessarily refer to the end of the world. We will see that Christ is making use of prophetic language.

If we turn to Daniel 12:1, we read: "At that time shall arise Michael, the great prince who has charge of your people. And there shall be a time of trouble, such as never has been since there was a nation till that time." Daniel is prophesying here about the time when the old covenant would end, that is, the time when Antiochus Epiphanes would oppress the Jews in a terrible manner. We find an account of Antiochus's rise to power, his outrageous rule, and his undoing in the preceding chapter (Dan. 11:21-45). .

Let's also look at Joel 2:2:

> A day of darkness and gloom, a day of clouds and thick darkness! Like blackness there is spread upon the mountains a great and powerful people; their like has never been from of old, nor will be again after them through the years of all generations.

Joel's prophecy concerns a plague of locusts. A gigantic army of locusts will appear, like blackness upon the mountains, a numerous and mighty people. They will approach the city of Jerusalem after having devastated the countryside. Joel says that there has never been a multitude of locusts like it, nor will there ever be again. The same thing is said about the swarm of locusts in Exodus 10:14 that swept over Egypt. In this way Joel ties together the plague that will overcome Jerusalem with the earlier plague of locusts in Egypt.

These two passages of Scripture show us that Christ's words about a tribulation "such as has not been from the beginning of the world until now, no, and never will be" do not necessarily refer to a tribulation occurring just before the world ends. Daniel uses a similar expression to underline the severity of the time of trouble. Joel uses such words to point out that the plague of locusts will be as consuming as the earlier plague in Egypt. Both these events of which Daniel and Joel prophesy take place in a period which is not near the end of the world.

We must understand Christ's words about a great tribulation in a similar fashion. They stress the acuteness of the believers' oppression. This oppression will take place at a definite time, namely, in the years preceding Jerusalem's destruction in A.D. 70.[3]

The Close of the Age

In the final section of His prophetic address, Christ concerns Himself with the last part of the disciples' question: "What will be the sign of the close of the age?" He answers them in verses 29-31 with a description of revolutionary cosmic aberrations, the sign of the Son of man in heaven, and then the Son of man coming on the clouds of heaven with power and great glory, surrounded

---

3. We object to the projection of "the great tribulation" to the end time; people then see it as a "sign" that will occur before Christ returns. Consequently, the expectation of an immediate return ebbs, for, after all, the tribulation has not yet arrived. "The great tribulation" that characterized the time before Jerusalem's destruction was typical of what the New Testament church would have to endure time and again throughout the centuries. When Revelation 7:14 says, "These are they who have come out of the great tribulation," the use of the present participle for "come" in the Greek indicates that the coming out of the great tribulation goes on continuously. See S. Greijdanus, *Kommentaar Openbaring*, pp. 174-5, who writes: "This is no exclusive reference to a unique tribulation, such as the last persecution towards the end of the world . . . ."

The Church will always endure oppression, more severe at certain times than at others, and varying in nature according to place, country, or continent (see John 16:33; Acts 14:22; I Thess. 1:6; 3:3; II Thess. 1:4ff; I Pet. 4:12). Even John, far away on Patmos, shared in the tribulation (Rev. 1:9).

by His angels, who gather the elect from out of the whole world.

This cannot be a reference to a judgment which is executed within a certain length of time. Even though Christ refers back to many Old Testament prophecies, He here focuses on His return. He refers to Isaiah's proclamation of judgment upon Babylon (Is. 13:19) and Edom (Is. 34:5) and in verse 30 to the prophecy of Zechariah 12:10, which concerns the events of Pentecost in Jerusalem. In verse 30·Christ also refers to the prophecy of Daniel 7:13, which describes the Messiah's ascension to the throne. In spite of these references to past prophecy, Christ's words must be seen in the context of the prophetic perspective which we have discussed earlier. He telescopes the events in such a way that His return is in full view.

Christ seems to be saying that the destruction of Jerusalem is the end of the world. Jerusalem's fall ushers in the catastrophe that will devastate the whole world. Yet we know that the two events are separated from each other in time by many centuries. But Christ puts them in one perspective: it is one and the same judgment of God which strikes Jerusalem in A.D. 70 and which will strike the apostate world at the time of Christ's return.

It is striking that Christ says in verse 34, "Truly, I say to you, this generation will not pass away till all these things take place." The generation that heard Christ's words would experience all these things! The Bible counts a generation as 40 years. If we add 40 years to the time of Jesus' death, we arrive at the year of Jerusalem's destruction: this generation would experience all the things that would accompany that destruction.

No, this generation did not experience the end of the world. Christ did not say that. "All these things" refers to the destruction of the city, which, when seen in prophetic perspective, ushers in the destruction of the world. The close of the age, or the consummation, is in principle embedded within the destruction of Jerusalem.

The Lesson of the Fig Tree

Whoever disregards the fact that Matthew 24 concerns the downfall of Jerusalem in A.D. 70 and that the end of the world figures here only in conjunction with it has lost the key to a correct understanding of Jesus' prophetic address. Hal Lindsey does just that. His mistake results in bizarre speculations; his "application" of the lesson of the fig tree is a prime example of such speculation.

Christ says, "From the fig tree learn its lesson: as soon as its branch becomes tender and puts forth its leaves, you know that summer is near. So also, when you see all these things, you know that he is near, at the very gates" (vs. 32-3 RSV). The Savior hereby tells the disciples that they will be able to know when the downfall of Jerusalem is imminent. Just as the appearance of the first leaves on the fig tree will indicate the approach of summer, so the appearance of the things Jesus foretold will indicate that the downfall of Jerusalem is near.

How does Lindsey interpret this lesson of the fig tree? He claims that the establishment of the Jewish nation on May 14, 1948 is comparable to the sprouting of the first leaves of the fig tree. What does he then do with Christ's words that this generation shall not pass away until these things take place? He says that "this generation" refers to the generation that witnesses the predicted signs, of which the rebirth of Israel is by far the most important.

Once more Lindsey busies himself with calculations.

He writes: "A generation in the Bible is something like forty years. If this is a correct deduction, then within forty years or so of 1948, all these things could take place" (PE, 43). But this is nothing more than speculation! It shows how far afield one can go by disregarding the fact that Christ was speaking to His disciples about the destruction of Jerusalem in A.D. 70, and the events which would precede it.

What, then, does Matthew 24 have to tell us? Exactly the same message that Christ gave the disciples: watch, therefore! But whereas Christ informed the disciples of the precise order of the events preceding the destruction of Jerusalem, He does not give us such information about the events before His return. Whereas He told the disciples that the present generation would experience these things, He does not tell us which generation will witness His return. The destruction of Jerusalem occurred in A.D. 70; we only know that Christ's return lies beyond it.

Learn the lesson of the fig tree! For us it means: Be aware that we live in the end times, and that Christ is making haste to return. Without being guilty of calculation, we are able to read Christ's haste in the events of our time. A particularly telltale sign is the present apostasy which is predicted in many parts of Scripture. We can clearly see that we live in the end times in that the apostasy which has beset the Church throughout her history is now approaching a climax.

In our time there is an alarming lack of eschatological insight; missing is the awareness that the end of all things is near and that Christ is coming with haste. Consequently, we don't know how to live in an eschatological manner. The expectation of Christ's coming is not part of our day-to-day living, as it should be. We must watch, even though we don't know whether

He will come in our time, and we may not speculate about it.

"Watch at all times," says Christ, "praying that you may have strength to escape all these things that will take place, and to stand before the Son of man" (Luke 21:36). Does this mean that we should pray for death to take us before Christ returns? Certainly not. Rather, we are to pray that we will still be here to witness Christ's return on the clouds.

Terrible things will happen before Christ consummates world history: signs in the sun and moon and stars, desperation among the nations. But the believers need have no fear. Scripture says that those who belong to Christ will be taken up in the clouds to meet the Lord in the air (I Thess. 4:17).

Finally, let us be on our guard against speculations about "wars and earthquakes," as if they are specific agenda items to be ticked off before Christ returns. These calamities did have a definite place on the agenda for the destruction of Jerusalem, but that is not the case with respect to Christ's return. Besides, Christ has not revealed to us the sequence of the times on His return agenda. Wars and earthquakes as such do not function as signs of the approaching end, because they have occurred throughout history.[4]

---

4. As far as the twentieth century is concerned, we can point to various earthquakes. On April 18, 1906, San Francisco was devastated. On December 28, 1908, tidal waves claimed 100,000 lives and destroyed Messina, Reggio and other places. On August 31, 1923, the Japanese earthquake which struck Tokyo and Yokohama killed 150,000 people. But earthquakes also occurred during the Old Testament period. An earthquake occurred in Palestine during the reign of Jeroboam II, king of Judah, in approximately 770 B.C. (see Amos 1:1). This earthquake was so severe that the people fled to escape it (Zech. 14:5). In the New Testament, earthquakes occurred when

The book of Revelation does mention earthquakes, but not in the usual sense. People use the occurrence of an earthquake as an occasion to claim that Christ will surely return very shortly. But the point in Revelation is that these catastrophic events reveal the anger of God over the apostasy of the world. These judgments of God, which have always been part of world history, will continue until the end, and they will accompany Christ's appearance (see Rev. 6:12; 11:13,19; 16:18).

According to Revelation 8:3ff, these judgments are at the same time answers to the prayers of the saints. When the angel filled the censer with fire from the altar and threw it on the earth, there were peals of thunder, loud noises, flashes of lightning, and an earthquake.

In this way we learn what to expect when we pray to God "for everything he has commanded us to ask for" (Heidelberg Catechism, Answer 119). We may not pray for peace and liberty simply as gifts for us to enjoy. We must pray for them in the context of the hallowing of God's name, the coming of His Kingdom, and the sovereign execution of His will. Then we will know that our redemption is being accomplished in the midst of the judgments.[5]

Christ died (Matt. 27:51), when Christ arose (Matt. 28:2), and also when Paul and Silas were in prison in Philippi (Acts 16:26).

5. Isaiah 26:8. Here, too, God's name and reputation are central, as can be seen in the second part of the verse: "Thy memorial name is the desire of our soul." That God makes level the path of the righteous (26:7) does not mean that everything will go smoothly. The believers pray that the Lord will magnify His name and His glory, all the while knowing that the Lord comes in the path of judgments. But even in that path the Lord will make the path of the righteous level, that is to say, they will reach their destination of complete redemption. In this way God's people can wait for the Lord in the path of His judgments.

7

Zechariah's Prophecies about Jerusalem

Lindsey writes:

> Another important event that had to take place
> before the stage would be fully set for the "seven-year
> countdown" was the repossession of ancient Jerusalem.
> Much of what is to happen to the Jewish people at the
> return of the Messiah is to occur in the vicinity of the
> ancient city.
>
> Zechariah some 2500 years ago predicted the great
> invasion against the Jewish people who would dwell
> near ancient Jerusalem at the time of Messiah's second
> coming. Chapters 12 through 14 of Zechariah graphi-
> cally describe the events in sequence (PE, 43-4).

After a six-point outline of these chapters, Lindsey
continues with:

> It is clear in these chapters that the Jews would have
> to be dwelling in and have possession of the ancient
> city of Jerusalem at the time of the Messiah's trium-
> phant advent.

Before we look at Zechariah 12-14, we should pay
attention to Zechariah 8:7-8:

> Thus says the Lord of hosts: Behold, I will save my
> people from the east country and from the west coun-
> try; and I will bring them to dwell in the midst of
> Jerusalem; and they shall be my people and I will be
> their God, in faithfulness and in righteousness.

Our first concern is the historical framework of this
prophecy. Zechariah began to prophesy in 520 B.C., in
the second year of King Darius (see Zech. 1:1), who
reigned 521-486 B.C. In 420 Zechariah saw visions that
comforted and encouraged the disheartened returned
exiles, who just couldn't seem to get a good start on the
building of the temple. Zechariah's job was to get the
Jews to work on the temple. He succeeded, and in 4 1/2
years the temple was completed.

In the later historical developments, Darius was succeeded by his son Xerxes I (who is the king found in the
book of Esther). The successor of Xerxes I was Artaxerxes
I (465-424 B.C.). During his rule the Jews were again
troubled by their adversaries. In 458, in the seventh year
of his rule, Artaxerxes gave Ezra permission to return to
Jerusalem with a number of other exiles. Thirteen years
later this same king sent Nehemiah to Jerusalem. This
would have been in 445. This means that 75 years elapsed
between the beginning of Zechariah's prophecy and the
second return out of Babylon.

Now we can understand that Zechariah's prophecy
in 8:7-8 is a promise of return out of exile. It will not be a
return at the end of the ages but one 75 years after
Zechariah begins to prophesy. We shouldn't look very far
for the fulfillment of this prophecy. For that matter, it
does say in Zechariah 8:15 that God will fulfill His
promise "in these days."

Zechariah is therefore prophesying about a second
return from Babylonian exile, under the leadership of

isn't there a fulfillment of the prophecy in the story of the return of God's people out of exile? We must also look for a possible further fulfillment of everything that is prophesied in this oracle.

What exactly is meant by "on that day"? It is the day or time of redemption. Because it indicates the several dimensions of God's redemption, we must see this day in a larger sense than simply the end of the world or the day of Christ's return. This will become evident in the prophecy of Zechariah: God's salvation begins to take shape in post-exilic Jerusalem, it continues in the Church of Christ throughout her history, and it is consummated in the New Jerusalem.

Zechariah 12:1-9

In this first section of chapters 12-14, Lindsey sees the following: the siege of Jerusalem by all nations (vs. 1-3) and a description of the battle in and around Jerusalem (vs. 4-9). By Jerusalem Lindsey means the city where the Jews will be living near the end of the world, when the Messiah returns. Accordingly, he says that the siege and battle spoken of here will take place just before Christ's return.

Zechariah 8:7-8 has shown us the error of this view. When Zechariah prophesies about people again living in Jerusalem, he is not speaking of present-day Jews but of those Jews who returned out of Babylonian exile. That includes the first group who came with Jeshua and Zerubbabel as well as those who came back 75 years after Zechariah's prophecy, in the time of Ezra and Nehemiah.

Zechariah concerns himself with what happens to Jerusalem and to the returned people of God. The nations rush upon Jerusalem and besiege it. But victory is harder

Ezra and Nehemiah. The objection might b
according to Zechariah 8:7, the Lord saves Hi
only from the east country but also from the
try. We need only remember that the prison
were often sold as slaves and would wind i
western Greek territories via the merchants.

This prophecy gives comfort to those who
turned with Jeshua and Zerubbabel. They were
small group; what could they hope to accomplish?
riah encourages them with the promise that their
ers, who are still in exile, will come to strengthen t
The Lord will find the exiles everywhere and bring t
to Jerusalem, where they will again live.

We can find a further fulfillment of this prophecy
the fact that Christ, through His Spirit, dwells with I
Church in faithfulness and righteousness. The earth
city of Jerusalem never fully became the city of faith
fulness and righteousness. The promise is being fulfilled
in the Church of Christ, and will ultimately be fulfilled in
the New Jerusalem. Then God will dwell with men, they
shall be His people, and He will be with them (Rev.
21:3). Nothing unclean and no one who practices
abomination or falsehood will enter that New Jerusalem
(Rev. 21:27). It will be a city of faithfulness and
righteousness.

Before beginning a section-by-section analysis of
Zechariah 12-14, We must take a look at the expression
"on that day" which constantly appears in those chapters.
It is often seen as the day of Christ's return, or, a little
more freely, as the end of the world.

It is not correct to narrow down Zechariah's
prophecies in such a way that they relate only to the end
of the world, as the headings in some Bibles suggest. We
must ask ourselves: To what, in the first place, does the
Word of the Lord concerning Israel (Zech. 12:1) relate?

to come by than expected, because the Lord lives in Jerusalem and He won't stand for it. He makes Jerusalem to be "a cup of reeling" to all the peoples. The enemy is like a drunkard who rushes upon the bottle of whiskey only to find that it stupefies and debilitates him. Similarly, the attack on Jerusalem will exhaust and weaken the nations. The Lord also makes Jerusalem to be a heavy stone that the attacking nations must raise. The strain of lifting it grievously hurts them.

Zechariah sees the nations coming together to engage in battle with Jerusalem, and he sees horses charging. The Lord strikes the horses with panic, their riders with madness, and then the horses with blindness. The Hebrew words for panic, madness, and blindness all end in a dull monotone, emphasizing the lack of force in the charge. It is clear that the attacking battle force is incapacitated.

But the Lord keeps His eye on His people. He repulses the whole attack. That does not mean that people are not involved. Verse 5 talks about the clans of Judah, which include Jerusalem. They acknowledge that their strength lies not in horses or chariots but in the Lord of hosts, the God of Israel's battle order. Because of this acknowledgment, the Lord strengthens the combatants and the clans of Judah so that they are invincible. They devour their enemies as would a blazing pot in the midst of wood and a flaming torch among sheaves. The Philistines found out what this meant when Samson chased the foxes with burning torches into the standing grain. It became a sea of fire; everything was destroyed.

And so the Lord saves Jerusalem. The triumph sounds in verse 6: "Jerusalem shall still be inhabited in its place, in Jerusalem." It might seem superfluous to say that Jerusalem will still be in Jerusalem. But it underlines the miracle that took place when the city did not succumb to the enemy's raging attack. The prophetic jubilation that Jerusalem would remain in its own place should not surprise us.

Verse 7 expresses that God alone is to be praised for this: "And the Lord will give victory to the tents of Judah first, that the glory of the house of David and the glory of the inhabitants of Jerusalem may not be exalted over that of Judah." Jerusalem may not exalt itself above the surrounding country; it must not boast of the greater safety that it, as a city, offers as compared with Judah. The Lord deserves all the glory for the deliverance.

The Lord will be a shield to the inhabitants of Jerusalem. The feeble ones among them will become mighty heroes like David. They will all become hardy and courageous, because the Lord will not eliminate any of His people. Every one of them will fight in the power of the Lord. Then the house of David will be "like God"; this latter phrase could also be translated "as heavenly beings." The supernatural power that they receive will make even the weakest as invincible as heavenly beings, and as the angel of the Lord that had given Israel victory over all its enemies (Ex. 23:23; Josh. 5:13ff). The Lord says in the final verse of this section: "And on that day I will seek to destroy all the nations that come against Jerusalem."

To what might this oracle relate? Imagine the setting that Zechariah is projecting. The Jews have returned out of exile. The second group, with Ezra and Nehemiah, have also returned. God's people are again centered around Jerusalem.

Did a battle occur in the time following the return? Yes, to be sure! There is only one conflict which is worthy of consideration in this context, namely, the fierce war that Antiochus Epiphanes waged against Jerusalem and the people of God. This occurred in about 167 B.C., 350 years after Zechariah prophesied, and 280 years after the Jewish exiles were reunited in Jerusalem. The Syrian King Antiochus Epiphanes had many allies to help him fight against Israel. The Jews, under the leadership of the Maccabees, fought fiercely and bravely against this huge army. Jerusalem remained "inhabited in its place."[1]

Did this complete the fulfillment of the prophecy? Not at all.[2] In this prophetic perspective we see the Lord protecting His Church throughout all the centuries against the ungodly forces that are set on her downfall. Today God's Jerusalem is the Christian Church. The heavenly Jerusalem is our mother (Gal. 4:26). We are come to the city of the living God, the heavenly Jerusalem (Heb. 12:22). That city can withstand all attacks! The Lord preserves His Church in the face of the raging of the whole world, even though she sometimes for a while appears very small, reduced to nothing in the sight of men.

---

1. According to G. C. Aalders, "One must think here of the protection of the Jewish people after the return from Babylonian exile, in the days of Antiochus Epiphanes" (*Het Herstel van Israel volgens het Oude Testament*, Kampen, no date, p. 246).

2. J. Ridderbos writes, "Here, too, we must look a little further. The fact that all the nations of the world come up against Jerusalem in verse 3 indicates the prophet's concern with something greater than just the Judean capital city: it is the Kingdom of God and the kingdom of the world that are pitted against each other here" (*Het Godswoord der profeten*, IV, Kampen, 1941, p. 929). Hellmuth Frey is somewhat more concrete. When it comes to the further fulfillment of Zechariah's prophecy about Jerusalem, he thinks in terms of the Church of Christ and observes "that the destiny of the nations is determined by the position they take over against Jerusalem, the Church of God, and that those who lay a hand on Jerusalem are judged by God" *(Das Buch der Kirche in der Weltende*, in the series "Die Botschaft des Alten Testaments," p. 312).

And on the last day God will definitively destroy all those who rise up against Jerusalem (Rev. 20:7-10).

Lindsey says that Zechariah 12:10 tells how Jesus Christ, at the time of His return, will personally reveal Himself as the Messiah to the Jews who are then living in Jerusalem. Verses 11-14 tell of the repentance and faith which result from this revelation.

Zechariah 12:10 states: "And I will pour out on the house of David and the inhabitants of Jerusalem a spirit of compassion and supplication, so that, when they look on him whom they have pierced . . . ." This means that they will pay attention to Him whom they had despised and rejected. Their eyes will have been opened. According to Lindsey, this will happen at the time of Christ's return. He evidently relates the words "they look on him whom they have pierced" to Revelation 1:7: "Behold, he is coming with the clouds, and every eye will see him, every one who pierced him."

It is correct to relate these two passages. However, it is incorrect to ignore an earlier fulfillment of this prophecy, a fulfillment of which the Scriptures themselves speak. When John in his gospel describes how a soldier pierced Jesus' side, he states that this is a fulfillment of the passage: "They shall look on him whom they have pierced" (John 19:37).[3]

Zechariah adds that they, that is, the whole nation, will mourn for Him as one would mourn for an only child or for a first-born who had died. The lamentation will be as great as the lamentation for Hadadrimmon in the plain

---

3. The fulfillment of Zechariah's prophecy includes more than the mere event of a soldier's piercing Jesus' side with a spear. According to J. Ridderbos, a deeper resonance lies in the lack of appreciation that Christ was shown by His people (*Het Godswoord der profeten*, IV, p. 300).

of Megiddo. This may be a reference to the annual lamentation for Josiah.

God's people will mourn when the Spirit of compassion and supplication moves them to realize what they have done by piercing Christ. At the time of the crucifixion they only saw Him in a physical sense, but on the day of Pentecost the Holy Spirit opened their eyes and hearts to the sin they had committed in piercing Jesus. This resulted in their cry of dismay: "Brethren, what shall we do?" (Acts 2:37).

We may not relate Zechariah's prophecy directly to Christ's return as Lindsey does, because the Scriptures clearly show that the prophecy is fulfilled in several stages. The first stage occurred when Christ was crucified. Another followed with the outpouring of the Holy Spirit on Pentecost. The prophecy is also fulfilled every time the New Testament church repents of her sins during the course of her history. The ultimate fulfillment will take place on the great day of the return of Jesus Christ on the clouds of heaven. Then all the tribes of the earth will wail on account of Him (Rev. 1:7). The believers will experience repentance as they see Him, and the unbelievers will experience remorse for having rejected Him who then comes to judge.

Zechariah 13:1-6

Lindsey only looks at verse 1 of chapter 13, which he sees as "the opening of the fountain of forgiveness to repentant Israel." Thinking exclusively of the time of Christ's return, Lindsey again does not do full justice to Zechariah's prophecy.[4]

---

4. This verse is definitely connected to the preceding section,

In this section of chapter 13, Zechariah prophesies about a time of redemption for the faithful, a time in which a fountain will be opened. The water from this spring washes away the guilt of sin. This should not lead us to think of something that will happen to a "repentant Israel" at the time of Christ's return. Rather, this comforting prophecy is directed to the New Testament church at all times. As the apostle John says, "The blood of Jesus his Son cleanses us from all sin" (I John 1:7). But Christ not only cleanses us; He also purifies us. The Spirit that was poured out on the Church on the day of Pentecost sanctifies the believers, causing them to break radically with sin. Zechariah mentions three sins that time and again brought a lot of trouble to the Church of the old covenant: the idols, the false prophets, and the unclean spirit that possessed the prophets.

A conversion takes place: the images of the idols are eradicated, and the false prophets are removed. Anyone still appearing as a prophet in a hairy mantle (the prophetic uniform) will be pierced by his parents according to the commandment of Deuteronomy 18:20. As a result, no one will again dare to pose as a prophet. The former prophet will say: "I am no prophet, I am a tiller of the soil." If someone then reminds him of his former position by asking about the wounds on his back that he had inflicted upon himself during a prophetic ecstasy (in the manner of the cutting with swords and lances by the

---

Zechariah 12:10-14. See J. Ridderbos, *Het Godswoord der profeten*, IV, p. 303: "The outpouring of the Spirit and the resulting inner renewal and inclination of the hearts to the One who was pierced is part and parcel of what is promised here: a gushing fountain to cleanse the house of David and the inhabitants of Jerusalem from sin and uncleanness."

priests of Baal on Mount Carmel), he will pretend they were caused by a fight with his comrades.

Christ's blood and Spirit bring about this kind of radical change, which is also repeatedly seen in the history of the New Testament church. With every reformation of the church, God destroys the unclean spirit, the devil, the false prophecy, and the idolatry. Then the Holy Spirit effects the miracles of repentance and renewal.

Zechariah's prophecy will ultimately be fulfilled on the day of Christ's return. Then the beast, the false prophet, and even the devil himself will be thrown into the lake of fire and brimstone (Rev. 19:20; 20:10).

Zechariah 13:7-9

It is striking that Lindsey fails to mention the prophecy about the shepherd that was struck and the sheep that were scattered. Did he perhaps find that his views are in conflict with this passage? After all, Jesus emphatically declared that this prophecy of Zechariah was being fulfilled in His time when He said to His disciples: "You will all fall away because of me this night; for it is written, 'I will strike the shepherd, and the sheep of the flock will be scattered'" (Matt. 26:31 RSV). The prophecy was fulfilled when Jesus died a violent death and when the disciples "fell away" at the time of His arrest. In this scattering of the sheep, God was disciplining His people for their lack of faith. The judgment applies to the unfaithful ones of Zechariah's time as well as to the fleeing disciples.

But that is only a part of the fulfillment. Zechariah prophesies that with the death of the shepherd and the scattering of the sheep, judgment comes, but through it appears a renewed and purified people of God. Then the time of redemption begins. Those remaining, those who have been purified in the crucible, call on the name of the Lord, and God answers them. The Lord recognizes them as His own; He calls them "My people." They in turn confess, "The Lord is my God."

In the old dispensation, judgment and purification involve a stripping away of part of the *nation.* Zechariah says that in the whole land, two thirds shall perish and one third shall remain. The remainder, who are purified by suffering and are again accepted as God's people, live in Canaan. The fulfillment of this prophecy makes it apparent that Christ's death brings an end to the national character of redemptive revelation.

The death of the Shepherd ultimately signified the preservation of the sheep. We are dealing here with the miracle of the substitutionary atonement. The sheep deserved the judgment of God. They should have been struck and killed, but instead the Good Shepherd, Jesus Christ, bore the judgment and the sheep were saved. They recognize the Lord as their God, and the Lord recognizes them as His people.

The fruit of the vicarious death of Christ on the cross will be tasted throughout the ages by those who "remain," those whom the Shepherd calls to Himself. On the last day, Christ will return to gather the sheep together so that there will be one flock and one Shepherd. Then God and His people will be eternally united.

Zechariah 14:1-21

Lindsey reads chapter 14 as a description of the Messiah's triumphant return, occurring in the end times when the Jews once again live in the city of Jerusalem. It will be helpful for us to first look at chapter 14:1-11. Zechariah sees all the nations gathered together to do battle against Jerusalem. The city capitulates. The conquerors commit terrible atrocities.

This is no ordinary battle. The text emphatically states that it is the Lord who gathers these nations against Jerusalem. We should note verse 4: "On that day his feet shall stand on the Mount of Olives which lies before Jerusalem on the east." This is similar to Ezekiel 11:23: "And the glory of the Lord went up from the midst of the city, and stood upon the mountain which is on the east side of the city."

Ezekiel saw the Lord departing from Jerusalem. The glory of the Lord left the city and settled on the mountain to the east of the city, that is, on the Mount of Olives. Then Jerusalem's fate was sealed. The city would be taken, and its inhabitants would go into exile. Zechariah also mentions the Mount of Olives on which the feet of the Lord stand. That literally took place when Christ, in whom the royal glory of the Lord had been revealed, ascended to His throne in heaven.

And so the glory of the Lord left Jerusalem a second time. That means that Jerusalem was approaching another fall. This happened about forty years later, in A.D. 70. Then the Lord Jesus judged Israel, letting its enemies destroy the city.

Many people see this as an eschatological prophecy. This plays right into Lindsey's hand; he agrees with them and goes one step further, saying that the references to Jerusalem and the Mount of Olives are to be taken literally. But others avoid this conclusion by taking these references as the Old Testament colors of the prophecy.

But why is the Mount of Olives specifically mentioned? On the basis of the reference to the Mount of Olives in Ezekiel 11, we may assume that here, too, the prophet is dealing with the glory of the Lord that is departing from Jerusalem. In that case the initial fulfillment of the prophecy took place when Jesus was forcibly taken from Jerusalem and when He ascended from the Mount of Olives. Zechariah's prophecy about the battle of the nations is certainly described in eschatological terms, but an earlier fulfillment need not be denied.

The prophecy continues. The Lord comes graciously to deliver the rest of His people (vs. 2). Just as He had done so often in the past, the Lord now marches out to fight against the enemy. The Lord is a military hero who hastens to help His battered people.

For the fulfillment of this prophecy, we should first look to the ascension, when Christ departed and left behind the small group of disciples who returned to Jerusalem. But He did not forsake the small, feeble Church. On Pentecost He sent His Spirit to equip that small army with the power to engage in battle. The disciples didn't have an easy time of it in Jerusalem, but the Lord fought for them, making sure that they were able to escape the judgment of Jerusalem. Zechariah describes this graphically: contact with the feet of the Lord splits the Mount of Olives through the middle, creating a valley of escape for "the rest of the people." (This is an eschatological description of an earthquake. Biblical prophecy often links the intervention of the Lord with an earthquake, e.g. the prophecy of Ezekiel 38:19ff.)

God's people escape judgment. The Lord then turns on the enemy and destroys them (vs. 12-15). Does this exhaust the prophecy of Zechariah? Of course not. What Zechariah describes, the battle against the Church, the oppression, but also the deliverance of the true believers and the destruction of the enemy, continues throughout the centuries.

Zechariah has the end of the centuries in sight when he says: "Then the Lord your God will come, and all the holy ones with him" (vs. 5). The Lord will come, surrounded by His holy angels, on the great day of never-ending light, a day which will be in stark contrast to the darkness of the close of history. The shining light of God's glory will fill the earth: "At evening time there shall be light."

Zechariah talks about this more explicitly in verses 8-11, where he describes how Jerusalem is the center of salvation and the high point of the surrounding countryside. This is a prophecy about the heavenly Jerusalem that comes down from God out of heaven (see Rev. 21:2).

"And the Lord will become king over all the earth." Zechariah sees this happening during the whole New Testament era, from the ascension of Christ to His return. He looks at this long historical road in one prophetic glance. According to verses 16-19, everyone who survives out of all the nations will go up to Jerusalem to celebrate the Feast of Tabernacles. We don't have to read this literally. It is an Old Testament way of saying that the Gentiles will also be included in the new covenant and will one day celebrate the fulfillment of the Feast of Tabernacles (Rev. 7:9ff).

Zechariah says that whoever does not go up to Jerusalem will not receive rain. This is fulfilled in the fact that whoever does not seek his salvation in Christ will not receive eternal life. Zechariah adds that everything to be found in Jerusalem and in Judah will be holy to the Lord. This refers to the New Jerusalem, where neither anything unclean nor anyone who practices abomination or falsehood shall enter.

8

Ezekiel's Prophecy about Gog

The fifth chapter of Lindsey's book begins as follows:

> The new State of Israel will be plagued by a certain pattern of events which has been clearly forecasted.
>
> Shortly after the restoration of the Jews in the land of Israel, an incredible enemy will arise to its "uttermost north." This enemy will be composed of one great nation which will gather around it a number of allies. It is this "Northern Confederacy" that is destined to plunge the world into its final great war which Christ will return to end (PE, 48).

In the fifth chapter Lindsey writes at length about Ezekiel's prophecy concerning Gog and its allies, who will fight with Israel (Ezek. 38-39). Lindsey does not mince words when it comes to identifying Gog: he entitles the chapter "Russia is a Gog."

The Time of the Prophecy's Fulfillment

Lindsey claims that the events predicted in Ezekiel 38-39 will take place shortly before the return of Christ. He points to the use of the expressions "the latter years" (38:8), and "the latter days" (38:16) to justify his claim: "These are definite terms which denote the time just preceding and including the events which will be climaxed by the second advent of Jesus Christ" (PE, 49). However, as we have learned in Chapter 2, we may not assume that "the latter days" refers to the end of the world.

Lindsey then calls our attention to the fact that the prophecy concerning Gog is found in the context of the final and permanent settlement of the Jews in Palestine (Ezek. 36-37). He says that this clearly does not refer to the return of the Jews from Babylonian exile. He gives several reasons. First, they are to return from a long, worldwide dispersion, whereas the Babylonian exile was neither long nor worldwide. We would reply that the length of the Babylonian exile was certainly not short. We need only remember how interminable the four or five years of German subjugation seemed to the people of occupied Europe during World War II to understand that the Babylonian exile seemed very long to the Israelites. As to the worldwide character of the dispersion, we have noticed earlier that the Jewish exiles were sold as slaves throughout the known world, and that therefore the prophecy does indeed apply to their situation.

Secondly, Lindsey argues that the restoration is to take place immediately prior to the period of tribulation: "This period brings about a great spiritual rebirth of the nation and the return of Jesus the Messiah to rescue them from their enemies" (p. 49).

It is undoubtedly true that Ezekiel is prophesying about the physical restoration of Israel (36:18). Its spiritual rebirth is also predicted:

> I will sprinkle clean water upon you, and you shall be clean from all your uncleannesses, and from all your idols I will cleanse you. A new heart I will give you, and a new spirit I will put within you; and I will take out of your flesh the heart of stone and give you a heart of flesh. And I will put my spirit within you, and cause you to walk in my statutes and be careful to observe my ordinances (36:25-7 RSV).

God repeats the ancient promise "You shall be my people, and I will be your God" (36:28). But all this does not prove that the physical and spiritual restoration of Israel will occur at the end of history just before Christ's return. The more plausible view is that Ezekiel's prophecy concerning the restoration of Israel refers to the events which occur after the return from Babylonian exile. This view does not imply that those events completely fulfill the prophecy, for after all, the promise of Israel's spiritual restoration is also fulfilled in the cleansing and renewing of the believers in Jesus Christ, by the blood of the covenant, by the pure water of baptism.[1]

---

1. The New Testament says that Christ cleanses His Church by His sacrificial death. He gave Himself for us, "to redeem us from all iniquity and to purify for himself a people of his own who are zealous for good deeds" (Titus 2:14 RSV). The words "to purify for himself a people of his own" are rooted in Ezekiel's prophecy about the restoration of Israel (Ezek. 37:23). In this way the New Testament interpretation shows us that we should relate the prophecies concerning Israel's future to the Church of Christ.

The New Testament does not apply the prophetic prediction of cleansing or purification to a Jewish nation of the end times but applies

According to Lindsey, the vision of the dry bones in Ezekiel 37 first describes the physical restoration of the nation, and then the spiritual rebirth of the people. The bones that again form a skeleton and are covered with muscles and tendons symbolize the physical restoration. Ezekiel's statement "But there was no breath in them" (37:8) tells Lindsey that the true, spiritual rebirth will only occur after the physical restoration of the nation. The spiritual rebirth will be the beginning of the eternal Kingdom of the Messiah. Lindsey backs this up with Ezekiel 37:26: "I will make a covenant of peace with them; it shall be an everlasting covenant with them . . . and [I] will set my sanctuary in the midst of them for evermore."

Does Ezekiel here really prophesy about a national, spiritual revival of the Jewish people just before the advent of the eternal Kingdom of the Messiah? If we look at the passage a little more closely, we will see that this is not the case. On the contrary, the vision of the revived bones is a symbolic proclamation of the return from exile. This is evident in verses 11-12:

> These bones are the whole house of Israel. Behold, they say, "Our bones are dried up, and our hope is lost; we are clean cut off." Therefore prophesy and say to them, Thus says the Lord God: Behold, I will open your graves, and raise you from your graves, O my people; and I will bring you home into the land of Israel.

---

it directly to the contemporary church of Christ, as in Titus 2:14. See also Ephesians 5:26 (Christ cleanses the Church by the washing of water with the Word) and Hebrews 9:14 (the blood of Christ purifies our conscience from dead works to serve the living God).

The Heidelberg Catechism echoes Scripture when it says that we are washed, that our sins are forgiven "because of Christ's blood poured out . . . in his sacrifice on the cross" (Answer 70).

"Graves" in verse 12 is a reference to the plight of
Israel at the time. Verse 11 expresses Israel's pessimism in
the face of her downfall: "Our bones are dried up and our
hope is lost; we are clean cut off." God's action of raising
them from their graves refers to the change in their condition that God will effect, namely, the return from
Babylonian exile. The text therefore does not speak about
the spiritual revival or the repentance of Israel just before
the end of the world.

Lindsey is also wrong when he distinguishes between
the physical and spiritual restoration of Israel on the basis
of Ezekiel 37. In the vision Ezekiel sees that the bones
that have been joined together still do not breathe (vs. 8).
Ezekiel must then command the breath to breathe upon
the dead, so that they may live (vs. 9). And so "the breath
came into them, and they lived, and stood upon their
feet." The action of the breath refers to nothing other
than that God, who is the God of the spirits of all flesh
(Num. 16:22), instils His life-giving Spirit within them
(see Gen. 7:22; Eccl. 12:7). The words "that they may
live" and "they lived" therefore do not refer to a spiritual
revival.

The question is whether verse 14 speaks of a spiritual
revival when it says: "I will put my Spirit within you, and
you shall live." Some say that this does indeed refer to a
religious renewal in Israel. But we must pay attention to
the unity of the vision (37:1-10) and its interpretation (vs.
11-14). In the interpretation, "I will put my Spirit within
you" is followed by the same words as we find in verses 8-
9: "that they may live." Therefore we must see the return
to life here also as the return from exile, which is the
theme of the whole vision. This is affirmed by the words
immediately following in verse 14: "and I will place you
in your own land."

The prophecy of Ezekiel 37 therefore symbolically

proclaims the return from exile in the vision of the dry
bones. This does not preclude the vision's foreshadowing
our deliverance from sin. As J. Ridderbos points out, "the
deeper sense of the prophecy about Israel's national
restoration is the great redemptive work of Christ, which
began with Christ's first coming and will be completed
with His second coming and the raising of the believers to
eternal life."[2]

Ezekiel 37 subsequently describes how the prophet
symbolically demonstrated the restoration of Israel's
unity. Ezekiel had to inscribe two sticks, one for the
kingdom of the two tribes and the other for the kingdom
of the ten tribes. Then he had to hold the two sticks in his
hand as if they were one stick. This showed that the Lord
would bring the people back from exile, and that He
would reunite them. The two kingdoms that had existed
since Rehoboam would again become one kingdom.

It is striking that verse 22 promises that the Lord will
cause one king to rule over them. Was this promise
fulfilled when they returned from exile in Babylon? We
should look closely at the text: "They shall be no longer
two nations, and no longer divided into two kingdoms."

This is what happened when they returned from
exile: there was one nation, ruled by one government.
Even though only a fraction of the ten tribes returned,[3]

---

2. *Het Godswoord der profeten*, IV, pp. 135-6.

3. There are people who insist that the return in 536 B.C. involved
only Judah, and not the ten tribes. This would mean that the prophecy
of Ezekiel was not fulfilled in the return from exile. There have been
all kinds of theories about what happened to the ten tribes, the most
popular one being that the ten tribes became the Anglo-Saxon race (the
British Israel movement). According to this view many of the promises
made to Israel were fulfilled in the British domination of the seas and
the British Empire.

their return marked the end of the split of David's kingdom: all the tribes were reunited, even though the house of David was not restored to the throne.

The Lord does promise a spiritual restoration in addition to the physical restoration: idolatry will end, and God again promises: "They shall be my people, and I will be their God" (vs. 23).

But there is more. This prophecy is not completely fulfilled with the return from exile. This is evident both from Titus 2:14, which applies Ezekiel's prophecy to the New Testament church, and from Ezekiel 37:24-8: "My servant David shall be king over them; and they shall all have one shepherd." Here we have a picture of Jesus Christ, the great David, who gathers the sheep. As He Himself said, "I have other sheep, that are not of this fold; I must bring them also, and they will heed my voice. So there shall be one flock, one shepherd" (John 10:16).

The one flock, gathered from Israel, from the Jews and from the Gentiles, will be a further fulfillment of Ezekiel's prophecy. The Lord will dwell in the midst of that flock; the Church will be His sanctuary.[4] Then

---

However, Scripture tells us that at least a small number of people from the ten tribes returned. Apparently some of those who had returned were not able to prove that they belonged to Israel (Ezra 2:59-60; Neh. 7:61-2). It must have been much easier for the people from Judah to give proof of their origins, since they had been in exile a relatively short time; those from Israel had been away for almost two centuries. In I Chronicles 9:3, we learn that some of the first inhabitants of Jerusalem after the return were from Judah and Benjamin, and also from Ephraim and Manasseh. Finally, people knew that the prophetess Anna came from the tribe of Asher (Luke 2:36).

4. In II Corinthians 6:16, the prophecy of Ezekiel 37:27 is applied to the body of believers, which is the temple of the living God.

In Ezekiel 37:24-8, we must not equate "sanctuary" with the temple of Zerubbabel, and "dwelling in the land" with the return from exile.

Israel's restoration will be complete. The nations will be impressed by Christ's work of gathering His Church.

The cause of the Church, which is now often defiled and persecuted, is in reality the cause of the Son of God. This will be fully evident when Christ returns. Ezekiel's prophecy will be completely fulfilled when the glory of the Lord beams forth as never before and the Lord establishes His sanctuary in the midst of His people, in the New Jerusalem. Then the dwelling of God will be with men, they shall be His people, and God Himself will dwell with them (Rev. 21:3).

The Leading Nation

We are now ready to look at the prophecy about Gog in Ezekiel 38-39. Lindsey says: "For centuries, long before the current events could have influenced the interpreter's ideas, men have recognized that Ezekiel's prophecy about the northern commander referred to Russia" (PE, 51). On what grounds does Lindsey base his claim? He refers us to Ezekiel 38:2, in which the leader from the north is described as "Gog, of the land of Magog, the chief prince of Meshech and Tubal."

Magog is mentioned in Genesis 10:2 as one of the sons of Japheth, together with, among others, Tubal and

---

In this instance the prophecy reaches beyond, to the time of Christ who blesses His people with His Messianic rule. However, it was not fulfilled in Christ's first coming because the temple was destroyed in A.D. 70 and the Jews were scattered across the world. The promises "I will set my sanctuary in the midst of them for evermore," and "They shall dwell in the land for ever" were not realized by the people of Israel in Canaan. Therefore we must see the land and the sanctuary as symbolic indications of the Church of Christ.

Meshech. Lindsey contends that the names *Magog*, *Meshech*, and *Tubal* have to do with contemporary Russia. He refers to such ancient historians as Herodotus, Josephus and Pliny. However, Lindsey's references to these writers do not prove that Gog should be identified with Russia.

Herodotus identified Meshech and Tubal with a people that lived in the ancient province of Pontus in northern Asia Minor at that time, says Lindsey (PE, 53). The other peoples of Ezekiel 38 were to be found in this same area, and not in Russia. Josephus identified Magog with the land of the Scythians. These people were Indo-European nomadic tribes who left their mark as a people of the steppes of southern Russia. It is important that we distinguish between the original and later residence of these people. What Josephus said about the descendants of Meshech and Tubal and about the later residence of the Scythians does not prove that the Biblical references to Meshech and Tubal are direct references to modern Russia. The same is true of what the Roman writer Pliny said.

Lindsey also calls on the nineteenth century Hebrew philologist Wilhelm Gesenius, who said that Meshech was the founder of the Moschi, a barbaric people who lived in the Moschian mountains. Apparently "Moschi" is the source of the name of the city of Moscow. Tubal was the founder of the Tibereni, a people who lived on the Black Sea to the west of the Moschi. According to Gesenius, modern Russian people are the descendents of these peoples.

However, scholars today generally agree that the names *Meshech* and *Tubal* have to do with the Mushki and Tabal, who appear in cuneiform writings. These are the Moschoi and Tabaleans that the Greek historian Herodotus mentions, who lived to the southeast of the Black Sea.[5]

But what does Magog refer to? It is not very easy to determine which region it indicates. We might get somewhere if we take into account that in Genesis 10:2 Magog is mentioned between Gomer (probably the Cimmerians) and Madai, that is, Media. Most likely its proper place on the map is somewhere between the coastal area of the Black Sea and the northern boundary of inland Media.[6]

Lindsey translates Ezekiel 38:2 as follows: "Gog, of the land of Magog, the chief prince (or ruler) of Rosh, of Meshech and Tubal." The name Rosh deserves special attention. Lindsey makes a direct connection between Rosh and Russ, or the Russian nation. He quotes Gesenius again: "Rosh was a designation for the tribes then north of the Taurus Mountains, dwelling in the neighborhood of the Volga" (PE, 54).

However, Rosh is no geographical designation and has nothing to do with Russ or Russia. Rather, it is a title, and the verse in question should be translated, as in the RSV: "Gog, chief prince . . ." and not:"Gog, prince of Rosh . . . ."[7]

---

5. G. C. Aalders, *Commentaar Ezechiël*, II, p. 115. Others have also referred to the tribes southeast of the Black Sea in Asia Minor. See J. Ridderbos, *Het Godswoord der Profeten*, IV, p. 158, footnote 2. W. Zimmerli refers to Ezekiel 27:13, where Meshech and Tubal are mentioned as trading partners of the great commercial city of Tyre; they were politically important powers "who would later once again employ their considerable power as a threat" (*Ezechiël*, p. 947). A. Noordtzij claims that these tribes lived in Phrygia and Cappadocia (*Ezechiël*, in the "Korte Verklaring" series, p. 122).

6. The name *Gog* is derived from the better known Magog, which was already mentioned in Genesis 10:2. We should therefore see Gog as someone originating in the land of Magog, or as someone who rules over that land.

7. There have been many attempts to identify Rosh with the tribe of

All the indications that we have found so far point us to the area southeast of the Black Sea and north of the land of Canaan. It is nothing more than fantasy to say what Lindsey says about the phrase "the uttermost north," from where the enemy originates: "You need only to take a globe to verify this exact geographical fix. There is only one nation to the 'uttermost north' of Israel—the U.S.S.R." (PE, 54). But we don't have to look so far afield to find the area of Gog. With respect to Palestine, the area southeast of the Black Sea is certainly "the uttermost north," and Gog did expand its sphere of power into the north.

The Allies

The allies of Gog are listed in Ezekiel 38:5-6: "Persia, Cush, and Put are with them, all of them with shield and helmet; Gomer and all his hordes; Beth-togarmah from the uttermost parts of the north with all his hordes." Lindsey has modern identifications for all of these allies. "Persia" is nothing other than modern Iran. "In order to

---

the Rhoxalani, an identification which pointed scholars to the Russians (see W. Zimmerli, *Ezechiël*, p. 947; A. Noordtzij, *Ezechiël* in the "Korte Verklaring" series, p. 122). However, there exists no historical basis for identifying Rosh with Russ; the only possible basis is the phonetic similarity between the two.

The translation of *nasi rosh* as "chief prince" finds a parallel in the translation of *kohen rosh* as "chief priest" (see II Kings 25:18; Ezra 7:5; I Chron. 27:5). Both "chief priest" and "chief prince" are titles. The latter title does not designate Gog as the ruler of one large kingdom but as the leader of several tribes (see Zimmerli, *Ezechiël*, p. 948).

mount the large-scale invasion predicted by Ezekiel, Russia would need Iran as an ally" (PE, 56). Lindsey also points to the friendly relations between Iran and Russia and the United Arab Republic.

Lindsey should not look at the contemporary world map, but instead at a map of the ancient Near East. Ezekiel was not prophesying about the Iran of our day nor about troop movements of the twentieth century; rather, he was prophesying about troop movements and alliances in the world of his time. In that context it is logical that the Persians were partners with Gog, for they were, just like Meshech and Tubal, Indo-European people, although they lived much farther to the south.

Ezekiel also mentions Cush, a word which may be translated as "Ethiopia." The Ethiopians were a people who lived south of Egypt. Relying on Gesenius's conclusion that all the black people were descendants of Cush, Lindsey extends the region of Cush to include all the black people of Africa. Then he goes on again to relate the prophecy to modern political reality: he says that many African nations will be united and allied with Russia in the invasion of Israel.

> The Russian force is called "the King of the North" and the sphere of power which the African (Cush) force will be a part of is called "the King of the South." One of the most active areas of evangelism for the Communist "gospel" is in Africa (PE, 57).

We can't accept such an "interpretation." "Cush" refers to the people who were living to the south of Egypt. Later we will consider how it was possible for such a southerly people to be allied with a power from the far north, and we will consider to which event this alliance refers.

With reference to the third ally, Put, Lindsey points out that Put was the third son of Ham, according to Genesis 10:6. He says that the descendants of Ham migrated to the area west of Egypt. The North African Arab nations, such as Libya, Algeria, Tunisia, and Morocco, developed from these people. And so he expands the notion of "Russia's ally, Put" to include much more than modern Libya: he includes the whole North African territory, which will join the southern sphere of power to attack Israel along with the "King of the North" (PE, 57-8).

Here, too, Lindsey's imagination plays tricks on him. Scholars do not agree on the designation of "Put." Some say it refers to the "Punt" which is to be found in Egyptian writings and which existed along the Red Sea across from the tip of Arabia. Others disagree, saying that "Put" refers to Libya, to the west of Egypt. Still others say that it is impossible to determine which region or people is designated by "Put." Even if we should decide that Libya is "Put," we would still not be justified in expanding the area to include all of the Arab-African countries, let alone in saying that the Bible here speaks about an alliance of the Arab-African countries with Russia against Israel.

Ezekiel next mentions the ally Gomer and all his hordes. Gomer is mentioned in Genesis 10:2 as the oldest son of Japheth and the father of Ashkenaz. Lindsey sees Gomer and all his hordes as the countries behind the Iron Curtain, the extensive area of eastern Europe, which includes East Germany and the Slavic countries. He quotes from Robert Young, who, by studying archaelogical findings, decided that Gomer and all his hordes "settled on the north of the Black Sea, and then spread themselves southward and westward to the extremities of Europe" (PE, 58).

To pinpoint Gomer and all his hordes on a map on the basis of their later residence is not a valid approach. Ezekiel was prophesying to his contemporaries and was naturally referring to their residence of that time. The question is: Where did they then live? In the Akkadian language, Gomer is *Gimirrai*, that is, the Cimmerians. It is impossible that Germany is to be understood here. Ezekiel is speaking about the Cimmerians of Cappadocia, who pushed into Armenia during the time of Sargon as well as after his time. This points us in a completely different direction. Cappadocia is located in southeastern Asia Minor, and Armenia is northeast of it and southeast of the Black Sea. This ally can therefore be located in the same general area as the other allies mentioned by Ezekiel.

The last ally that Ezekiel mentions by name is Togarmah, from the far north, with all his hordes. Lindsey learns from Gesenius that "some of the sons of Togarmah founded Armenia, according to their own claim today" (PE, 58-9). It's true that Togarmah is often identified with Armenia; this again locates it in the same general area as the other allies of Gog: southeast of the Black Sea.

But Lindsey does not leave well enough alone. By looking at the assertions of someone who traced some of the sons of Togarmah to the Turkoman tribes of central Asia, he concludes that "Togarmah is part of modern Southern Russia and is probably the origin of the Cossacks and other people of the Eastern part of Russia" (PE, 59).

Here again Lindsey uses a little bit of historical data (whose validity may be open to question) to draw the conclusion that Togarmah designates southern Russia and the Cossacks. He embroiders his conclusion by remarking that the Cossacks have the best army of

cavalry in the world, and that some military men believe
cavalry will be used in the invasion of the Middle East,
"just as Ezekiel and the other prophets literally predicted."

But Lindsey has not proved that Ezekiel is
prophesying about southern Russia and the Cossacks. It is
admittedly tempting when Ezekiel talks about horses and
riders to jump to the conclusion that he is referring to
southern Russia and the Cossacks and then to say, "See,
Ezekiel already prophesied about this long ago!"
However, conclusive arguments are lacking.

Another Interpretation

Who is Gog, and what is this prophecy really about?
We have seen that Ezekiel was prophesying about an armed
power to be found south and southeast of the Black
Sea. When will this force engage in the prophesied battle? Ezekiel must speak to Gog on behalf of the Lord. The
beginning of the prophecy is ominous: "Thus says the
Lord God: Behold, I am against you, O Gog, chief prince
of Meshech and Tubal."

Then Gog is informed that the Lord will lead his advance. Everything that this chief prince does is under the
control of the Lord. It is the Lord who commands Gog to
"be ready and keep ready, you and all the hosts that are
assembled about you, and be a guard for them" (Ezek.
38:7 RSV). The great commander Yahweh calls up Gog
to be ready for duty, to be ready to mobilize his huge army, an action which will end in his own destruction.

> After many days you will be mustered: in the latter
> years you will go against the land that is restored from
> war, the land where people were gathered from many

nations upon the mountains of Israel, which had been a continual waste; its people were brought out from the nations and now dwell securely, all of them (38:8 RSV).

This passage bears on the time after the exile. The expression "in the latter days," here as well as in Ezekiel 38:16, does not refer to the end of the world.[8] The end of chapter 39 ties together the Babylonian exile and the humiliation of Gog after the return from that exile. (Gog's humiliation and Israel's return demonstrate to the nations that Israel went into exile on account of her iniquity.) Therefore Gog is not an eschatological figure. He is a historical figure who appears "many days" after the exile but soon enough for the prophet to be able to relate the events to the people of his own time, for their composition and residence remained stable.

Gog advances with his allies. God commands him to do so, and Gog is more than willing. This is shown by God's words to Gog: "You will devise an evil scheme and say, 'I will go up against the land of unwalled villages; I will fall upon the quiet people who dwell securely' " (Ezek. 38:10-11). Gog is moved to action by the desire to seize spoil and carry off plunder. He will advance against a people who have been gathered from the nations and who have acquired cattle and goods. That refers to God's people, Israel, who by then have returned from exile, dwell in the waste places, and again possess cattle and goods. It is against this people that the Gentile nations, under the leadership of Gog, chief prince of Meshech and Tubal, advance.

---

8. Some scholars disagree, saying that this prophecy bears on the final struggle of history, when the forces of the Antichrist are destroyed during their last attack upon the Church (Rev. 20:7-10). It is also said that "in the latter days" is an eschatological reference to the time when the glory of the Messiah will descend upon Israel.

On the basis of the time indication ("many days" after the exile, 38:8), Israel's situation (vs. 11-12), and the geographical indications, we may assume that Gog and his allies refers to the Seleucids, in particular, to the Syrian king Antiochus Epiphanes IV (175-164 B.C.).

After Alexander the Great died, his mighty Greek empire was divided into several parts. The Seleucid dynasty managed to acquire a position of considerable power in northern Syria, extending its influence into Armenia and Asia Minor in the direction of the Black Sea. The center of Seleucid power was in northern Syria; the court capital was Antioch, located on the river Orontes. This corresponds exactly to the area to which Ezekiel's prophecy refers.

However, several of Gog's allies were to be found a considerable distance from this area. For example, Ezekiel mentions Persia. This isn't really so surprising, in that the influence of the Seleucids was extensive, and since the Persians also belonged to the Indo-European peoples. It might seem harder to explain how the Syrian king would be allied with Ethiopia and Put far in the south. But this becomes plausible when we consider that Ethiopia and Egypt were often at odds, and that "the king of the north" (Syria) was continually at war with "the king of the south" (Egypt) at that time. It is therefore logical that the Syrian king Antiochus Epiphanes would have received help from Ethiopia.

The situation described in Ezekiel 38:10-13 is another argument in favor of thinking of the war of Antiochus with the Jewish people. According to Ezekiel, his aim was to seize spoil and carry off plunder. Evidently there was plenty to be had from the Jews! That means that the returned exiles were again enjoying prosperity. This was not the case right after the exile, during the Persian period, but it was in the time of Syrian power.

It is especially important to notice the possible connection between verse 13 and an event of those days. That verse reads: "Sheba and Dedan and the merchants of Tarshish and all its villages will say to you, 'Have you come to seize spoil? Have you assembled your hosts to carry off plunder, to carry away silver and gold, to take away cattle and goods, to seize great spoil?'" The reference becomes clear when we take into account something which happened just before the Battle of Emmaus. The forces gathered against the Jews were so numerous that a Jewish defeat seemed inevitable. Then foreign merchants, eager for easy booty, joined the army of the Seleucids. They were anxious to sell the Jewish captives as slaves. Verse 13 may refer to these merchants.

We should note that the battle with Israel is described eschatologically: it makes us think of the end of the world. A major earthquake takes place, affecting fish, birds, the other animals, and men. The mountains are thrown down. Israel does not even need to enter into the battle, because panic breaks loose in Gog's army and they strike each other down. The Lord sends pestilence, hailstones, fire, and brimstone. It's as if the end of the world has come.

But that does not mean that this prophecy is primarily eschatological. Although certain characteristics of the description make us think of the end of time, we should first think of a concrete historical power that fought with Israel not so very long after Ezekiel uttered the prophecy.

We shouldn't forget that God is here pouring His anger out upon Gog. It is no small thing when God's anger is set ablaze. To describe the effect of the Lord's anger, the prophets often resort to eschatological terms. The wrath of the Lord makes the mountains totter and the earth to tremble.

Some scholars claim that since the things predicted in this prophecy did not occur during the time of Antiochus Epiphanes (or of any other great ruler), the prophecy must bear on the end of the world. We would reply that it is not necessary to look for a literal fulfillment of these events. Ezekiel often uses cosmic aberrations, events which do not literally come to pass, to describe God's intervention. In the prophecy about Egypt's judgment, the Nile is dried up and darkness comes over the land (30:12,18). In the lamentation about Pharaoh, the stars are darkened (32:7-8).

However, the prophecy of Ezekiel does not stand apart from what will happen during the consummation. God's judgment forms a unity, and it includes the judgment of Gog. Throughout history God will destroy the power of the Antichrist, and He will definitely do so during the consummation. Ezekiel's prophecy will not be completely fulfilled until fire descends from heaven to consume the nations from the four corners of the earth, that is, Gog and Magog (Rev. 20:7-10).

Ezekiel 39 predicts the sweeping defeat of Gog. The Lord leads him in his advance, and the Lord also crushes him. The Lord strikes the bows and arrows out of the hands of Gog's soldiers (vs. 3). This chief prince and his mighty force are utterly routed. Ezekiel uses hyperbolic language to describe this crushing defeat.

In connection with the destruction of Gog, Ezekiel says, "That is the day of which I have spoken" (39:8). This is probably a reference to the day of the Lord. But this still does not mean that we are dealing with the final judgment. The day of the Lord is expressed in every revelation of God's judging, punishing activity, which will fully and completely reveal itself in the final judgment.

We should of course not understand these things

literally, as, for example, when Ezekiel says that the weapons left on the battlefield will furnish the Israelites with enough firewood to last them for seven years. The same is true of the seven years it will take to bury the many victims of battle, and of the Lord's inviting the birds and beasts of prey to a sacrificial feast that He prepared for them on the mountains of Israel. This manner of speaking is simply used to emphasize how devastating Gog's military catastrophe was.

The prophecy doesn't necessarily say that Gog would be destroyed during a single, large battle. There are other places in the Bible where a series of events are described as a single act of war. For example, Jeremiah 4-6 and 8-9 describe the destruction of Jerusalem and the carrying off of the people into captivity as one act of the enemy, whereas in reality it took place in several stages. We may therefore also see the defeat of Gog as the result of a series of battles.

We can now conclude that the defeat of Gog refers to the complete dissolution of the power of Antiochus Epiphanes IV. This happened when the Jews, under the leadership of the Maccabees, utterly defeated the Syrian armies in a series of battles. The Syrian power had to give way to a handful of Jews. That was due to the intervention of God, who fought for Israel and destroyed the enemy on account of His fierce anger. In the same way, the Lord will continually stand up for His Church when she is oppressed by her enemies, all through the ages, until the end, when the enemy will be eternally destroyed.

9

Daniel 11 and Antiochus Epiphanes

The Bible says that Egypt, the Arabic nations, and countries of black Africa will form an alliance, a sphere of power which will be called the King of the South. Allied with Russia, the King of the North, this formidable confederacy will rise up against the restored state of Israel (PE, 61).

"The Bible says . . . ." Really? Where does Lindsey find that in the Bible? He refers us to Daniel 11, where Daniel calls Egypt "the king of the south." The first question we might ask Lindsey is which Egypt Daniel is talking about. Lindsey seems to be thinking of modern Egypt set in the contemporary world situation. According to him, recent events in the Middle East have set the stage for Egypt's last act in the drama which will climax in the personal return of Christ to earth (PE, 65). He bases this claim on what Daniel said about the "king of the south."

Lindsey does see fit to admit that Daniel 11 is concerned with the warfare between Egypt under the Ptolemaic dynasty and Syria under the Seleucid dynasty.

126

But that does not prevent him from saying that in verse 40, "Daniel leaps over a·long era of time to the events which lead up to the personal, visible appearance of Christ as God's righteous conqueror" (PE, 66). How does Lindsey arrive at this conclusion? Well, in verse 40 he reads the words "at the end of time," which, he says, "speak unmistakably of the beginning of the last great war of history." He continues by saying, "Daniel gives great detail concerning the battles and movement of troops which will take place at the beginning of this war."

This method of Scriptural interpretation is strictly arbitrary. We need to take a better look at the prophecy of Daniel 11.

Daniel 11

The reader of Daniel 11 is constantly plagued by the question: What is this all about? Things fall into place if we realize that this chapter is concerned with a part of history that begins in the time of Daniel and continues to the time of the wars between Egypt and Syria.

Let's look at Daniel 11:2: "Behold, three more kings shall arise in Persia; and a fourth shall be far richer than all of them; and when he has become strong through his riches, he shall stir up all against the kingdom of Greece." Since Daniel stayed in Babylon until the reign of Cyrus (see Dan. 1:21; 10:3), we should look for three kings after Cyrus. They are Cambyses, Darius I, and Xerxes I (Ahasuerus). Xerxes is the fourth king, and his riches will allow him to rouse the nations against Greece.

"Then a mighty king shall arise, who shall rule with great dominion and do according to his will" (vs. 3). The "mighty king" undoubtedly refers to the ruler of the Greek empire, Alexander the Great. The knowledgeable reader will notice right away that the prophecy skips over a large period of history: 130 years passed between Xerxes I and Alexander the Great. (Xerxes I ruled from 486-465 B.C. There were seven more kings who ruled over the Persian empire before Alexander established his world empire.)

Prophecy can skip periods in this way because it does not aim to relate all future events. This is the case even in the detailed predictions of Daniel 11. The prophecy fails to mention that there were several Persian kings after Xerxes. It was necessary to mention Xerxes because he was an important ruler who stirred up the conflict with Greece. Subsequently, according to the prophecy, Greece has its day in an equally imposing ruler, the ruler of the mighty Greek empire.

The prophecy continues: "And when he has arisen, his kingdom shall be broken and divided toward the four winds of heaven, but not to his posterity, nor according to the dominion with which he ruled; for his kingdom shall be plucked up and go to others besides these" (vs. 4). This part of the prophecy was fulfilled when Alexander died after an illness of ten days, at the age of 33. His immense empire was torn in pieces, just as Daniel had prophesied, and divided among his four great generals, the so-called Diadochi: Egypt went to Ptolemy, Syria to Seleucus, Macedonia to Cassander, and Thrace to Lysimachus.

Two of the new Diadochian kingdoms, the Ptolemaic dynasty of Egypt and the Seleucid dynasty of Syria, were constantly at war with each other. Daniel 11:5ff concerns the entanglements between the two nations. We will limit ourselves to making several observations about this section of the chapter.

Daniel here refers to the Ptolemaic dynasty of Egypt as "the king of the south" and to the Seleucid dynasty as "the king of the north." Secular history also tells us that these two dynasties were in constant conflict, the bone of contention being Palestine. The northern kingdom tried to extend its power and gain the upper hand, first by means of a political marriage and then by means of wars, but to no avail.

Then a new king appeared in the northern nation, a king who was able to acquire tremendous power. From verse 21 on, we read about this figure: "In his place shall arise a contemptible person to whom royal majesty has not been given; he shall come in without warning and obtain the kingdom by flatteries." This is a picture of a crafty schemer who usurps the throne from the legitimate heir. That can be none other than Antiochus Epiphanes!

The subsequent verses tell us that Antiochus is very successful in warfare, mostly on account of his deceitful intrigues. In verse 25 we learn that he is the aggressor and winner in a war against Egypt. He lies at the conference table like a true master of underhanded diplomacy (vs. 26-7). Finally he returns, laden with spoil, to his Syrian residence in Antioch.

In verse 28 we read the first suggestion of Antiochus's hatred for the Lord and His people: "His heart shall be set against the holy covenant." Antiochus simply can't stand the "holy covenant" between Yahweh and Israel. Secular history tells us that on his return from Egypt, Antiochus plundered Jerusalem. He entered the temple and took away the golden altar, the golden candlestick, the table of the showbread and its utensils, and other treasures. But this was only a foretaste of what God's people would have to endure at the hand of this terrible enemy.

Antiochus leads a second expedition against Egypt two years after the first. But this time his campaign fails.

The "ships of Kittim," coming from Greece,[1] force him to abandon his expedition (see vs. 29-30).

Defeat makes Antiochus furious. He takes out his anger on the Jews; on his return journey, according to Daniel, he would "be enraged and take action against the holy covenant" (vs. 30). He is ruthless in Hellenizing the Jews. He wants to put the stamp of Greek worship, culture and customs on the people of God. Sadly enough, he finds Jews who are susceptible to his propaganda, who are willing to renounce the "holy covenant" and to change their ways.

But a large number of the Jews do not succumb, and Antiochus retaliates. He sends a military force to wreak havoc in Jerusalem. The soldiers profane the temple, remove the continual burnt offering, and set up the abominable thing that causes desolation (vs. 31). This desecration of the temple in Jerusalem occurred when Antiochus changed it into a temple for the Greek god Zeus.

The Jews respond to these measures in two ways. Many of them forget about Yahweh and embrace Greek paganism. But others, who know their God, stand firm, and by their actions they demonstrate their faithfulness. The sword and flame, the captivity and plunder that they have to endure at the hand of the Syrians spur them on to even greater steadfastness.

Help arrives, according to verse 34. The prophecy here refers to the Maccabees, whose story is an interesting one. In the small town of Modin lived an old priest, Mattathias, who with his sons courageously resisted the

---

1. The Kittimites were originally the inhabitants of the Phoenician colony of Kition on Cyprus. In a wider sense "Kittim" refers to the Greeks and the other people living in the northern part of the Mediterranean basin. In this case the reference includes the Romans.

Syrians. Of the five sons, Judas became the leader of an armed rebellion. His courage earned him the title "the Maccabee," which means "the sledgehammer." Under the leadership of this family, a small group of poorly equipped, untrained fighters fought against the Syrians with unbelievable courage. They won, Antiochus's forces were sent packing, and the temple in Jerusalem was reconsecrated on December 25, 165 B.C.

Verse 36 reveals that self-idolization lies behind the hatred of Antiochus Epiphanes for God's people. He will exalt himself above every other god, Scripture tells us. Historical findings verify this, for on some of the coins of that time the depiction of Antiochus strongly resembles that of the god Zeus. One of the coins even bears the inscription "Of King Antiochus, the revealed god."

According to the prophecy, Antiochus will utter unprecedented words against the God of gods: he will flaunt his own exalted majesty before the most high God. He will pay no heed to the gods of his fathers but will devote himself fully to the service of Zeus and the Hellenistic religion, which he will force upon Israel.

The Final Period of Antiochus Epiphanes

"At the time of the end the king of the south shall attack him" (vs. 40). We have said earlier that Lindsey here skips over no small period of time to the events preceding Christ's return, and that his claim is strictly arbitrary. Why would Daniel suddenly switch from the Ptolemaic-Seleucid conflict to contemporary Egypt and Russia? How can Lindsey account for Daniel's continuing to use the same terms—"the king of the south" and "the king of the north"?

Lindsey argues that verse 40 says "at the time of the end." But that is no valid argument. "The time of the end" here refers to the end of the Ptolemaic-Seleucid conflict and the end of Antiochus himself. It is also significant that these events occur at the end of the Old Testament period of history.

According to verse 40, the two rivals will again attack each other. Lindsey totally misses the boat when he says that Egypt will attack the leader of the revived state of Israel, and that this leader will be a false Messiah, probably a Jew who will work closely with the world dictator of Rome (PE, 66). The passage gives no such indications. Even if we chose to ignore Lindsey's "end times" interpretation and his fantasy about the Jewish leader and the Roman dictator, we would still have to notice that the text does not say that Israel will be attacked. Rather, it says that the southern king will attack "him," meaning the king of the north, that is, Antiochus Epiphanes. There is no indication that "the king of the north" now suddenly refers to the leader of Israel.

According to Daniel 11, Antiochus seizes the opportunity created by the aggression from the south. With naval and ground forces, he swoops down on Egypt. In order to travel as quickly as possible, he uses the caravan highway through the coastal areas, and so "he shall come into countries and . . . pass through" (vs. 40). He also comes into "the glorious land," that is, Israel. He ignores the countries that do not lie along his route—Edom, Moab, and the main part of the Ammonites. In Egypt he finds the Libyans and Ethiopians, who were usually at odds with Egypt, ready to join him and enrich themselves. With their support Antiochus storms through Egypt, taking with him all the gold, silver and precious things that he can find.

Lindsey is again fantasizing when he claims, on the basis of the Libyan and Ethiopian support, "that the 'black African' and 'Arab-African' countries will be involved with Egypt and in line for Russian conquest as well" (PE, 67). That is simply not the meaning of the passage. We should instead here see Antiochus at the height of his power after his victory in Egypt.

But then news from the eastern and northern parts of his dominion alarms Antiochus. This news was about the invasion by the Parthians in the east and the rebellion in Armenia to the north. Antiochus quickly leaves Egypt. "And he shall pitch his palatial tents between the sea and the glorious holy mountain; yet he shall come to his end, with none to help him" (vs. 45). This means that Antiochus encamped on Jewish soil between the Mediterranean and Mount Zion before his life suddenly ended.

The text does not explicitly say that Antiochus died in Palestine. It only says that on his return he stopped in Palestine—after that his life came to an end. Scripture does not tell us where the latter event occurred. Secular history, however, says that Antiochus unexpectedly died from an illness during a campaign against the Parthians.

We must clearly reject Lindsey's interpretation of a formidable confederacy rising up against the restored state of Israel. Daniel 11 gives no support for it. This chapter is concerned not with the end times but with the end of the Old Testament period, when the Lord would deliver His people out of their dire distress. We can see a fulfillment of this prophecy in the protection that the Lord afforded His people during the perilous times of Antiochus's rule over them. With His help, they were able to endure.

With His help, the New Testament church, too, will continue to endure. God will protect His children against all hostile threats. That is the message of comfort to be found in Daniel 11.[2]

---

2. Paul makes use of Daniel 11:36 in his discussion of the man of lawlessness, who exalts himself against every so-called god or object of worship, and in the temple proclaims himself to be God (II Thess. 2:4). See Chapter 12 for more about this.

10

The Yellow Peril?

The Asian Horde in the Middle East

In the seventh chapter of this book, Lindsey tells us what the Bible, and in particular the book of Revelation, has to say about China during the end times. He gives the chapter a catchy title: "The Yellow Peril"!

In addition to Russia (the king of the north) and Egypt with its Arab-African alliance (the king of the south), a third power, from the east, now appears on the Middle East battle scene. Lindsey finds this new actor in Revelation 16:12: "The sixth angel poured his bowl on the great river Euphrates, and its water was dried up, to prepare the way for the kings from the east." The vast army will be able to advance from the east because the traditional boundary and obstacle between east and west, the Euphrates, will have been dried up.

Lindsey finds a further basis for his views in Revelation 9:14-16, where, after the release of the four angels at the river Euphrates, an army 200,000,000 strong turns up. This army, Lindsey says, will invade the Middle East. In 9:18 we read that it will wipe out a third

of mankind, using fire, smoke (or pollution), and brimstone (or melted earth). Lindsey suggests that all three
could refer to the effects of a future thermonuclear war.

He also says that this army will be raised up just
prior to Christ's return to earth (PE, 71). It is therefore of
great significance to Lindsey that China has already
begun to create the mighty force which John calls "the
kings of the east." The Chinese themselves are boasting of
being able to field a people's army of 200,000,000
soldiers. "In their own boast they named the same number as the Biblical prediction. Coincidence?" (PE, 75).
Lindsey also notes that by 1980 China will have ICBMs
capable of delivering H-bombs. "Within a decade China
alone will have the capacity to destroy one-third of the
world's population just as John predicted" (PE, 76). In
this way Lindsey tries to convince the reader that the picture for Christ's return is pretty well complete.

The Sixth Trumpet

Let's first look at Revelation 9:13ff. When the sixth
angel blows his trumpet, John hears a voice from the four
horns of the golden altar before God. In 8:3 we learned
that the incense of the prayers of all the saints rises from
this altar. The voices of the saints are like one mighty
voice calling on God to punish the apostate rejection of
His Word and will. The answer now comes, as the voice
of the Church becomes the voice of God commanding the
sixth angel of judgment to release the four angels bound
at the Euphrates River. This is the first mention of these
wicked angels who acted as satan's henchmen.

The Euphrates has a special significance in the
Bible. In his covenant with Abraham, God said, "To your

descendants I give this land, from the river of Egypt to the great river, the river Euphrates" (Gen. 15:18). It functioned as the boundary between the land of the Messiah and the Gentile lands, between the Kingdom of God and the kingdom of satan (see Ps. 72:8).

When the Israelites failed to distinguish the worship of Yahweh from the worship of the pagan gods around them, God broke down the barrier that had separated His people for centuries from the Assyrians and Babylonians who lived at the Euphrates River. He let the mighty Gentile powers sweep across the promised land to bring about the downfall of His people. God will do a similar thing again, according to Revelation 9. To punish mankind for its apostasy, He will let down the barrier between the people who once listened to the gospel and the powers of evil. The four angels of destruction will be released to deliver their deadly blows.

In our time, the Euphrates River is no longer the boundary between the domain of the Messiah and the domain of the pagan powers of the east. God no longer lives in the promised land, and the boundary of His Kingdom is not to be found at the Euphrates. Christ has come, and the wall of separation has been broken down. The Old Testament dispensation has passed. That's why Revelation 9 is not about Chinese forces crossing the Euphrates to wage war in the Middle east.

The four angels had been held ready for the hour, the day, the month, and the year (vs. 15). This indicates that God determines when the events of history will happen, and how long they will last. The angels are released to destroy one third of mankind, meaning that many will perish during this war. Scripture here shows that God judges the rejection of the gospel; He punishes those who refuse to heed the continual call to repentance. We should not relate this to a specific time, such as the end of the world. Rather, John is talking about the mighty struggle between Christ and satan, between the Kingdom of God and the kingdom of the evil one, a struggle that marks all of history.

A vast army appears. John hears the number of twice ten thousand times ten thousand. We shouldn't take this figure literally but should see it as a symbolic indication of the immensity of this horde. The war will be a terrible one.

Numbers mentioned in Revelation often have a symbolic significance. The number 7 appears frequently, but it does not always have the same significance. We read about "the seven spirits who are before his throne" in 1:4. Here the number 7 relates the spirits to the seven candlesticks in the tabernacle. It also symbolically indicates the fullness of the Holy Spirit's work. But in 8:2, where "the seven angels who stand before God" are mentioned, the number 7 has only a literal meaning.

In plurality the numbers 7 and 10 indicate a definite fullness. The number of the cavalry in Revelation 9 shows a symbolic system of numbers in which the number 10 plays a significant role: $10,000 \times 10,000 = 100,000,000$; twice that is 200,000,000.

The army that John sees is made up of cavalry only. The riders' breastplates are colored like the red fire, the blue smoke, and the yellowish sulphur that issue out of the horses' mouths. The heads of the horses resemble lions' heads. The power of the horses is in their mouths and tails, their tails being like snakes with heads. All these details tell us that this is no ordinary troop of cavalry but an army driven by satanic power. Other parts of Scripture relate the images here used—the first, the lion and the snake—to the devil and his hellish power.[1]

---

1. The smoke of fire brings darkness, and its brimstone suffocates.

None other than satan mobilizes these millions of people to effect a terrible devastation.

As we have said, this vision is not about a final battle of the nations but about the struggles that the Christian church has had to endure throughout its history, struggles whose horror and intensity are increasing. The history of Europe contains examples of this struggle. A massive attack on the Christian church and Christian culture took place when the pagan Turkish forces captured a large portion of southern Europe. Many centuries later, the Nazi armies sowed death and ruin as Hitler tried to establish the religion of race, blood and soil as the supreme religion. Today the apostate Communists control large parts of Europe.

In other parts of the world, we see China's power continuing to increase and Communism spreading in the Asian countries. In Africa, too, Communism is on the advance, and the non-Christian nations are growing in importance. We are therefore not saying that the demonic cavalry of Revelation 9 has nothing to do with China. But we fail to see a detailed description of Asian hordes fighting in the Middle East during the end times.

The Sixth Bowl

We should also look at Revelation 16, where Lindsey reads the coming of the Chinese armies in the reference to the Euphrates and the coming of "the kings from the east." What we said earlier about the Euphrates with respect to chapter 9 holds for chapter 16 also. The total

---

The devil prowls about like a roaring lion, seeking someone to devour (I Pet. 5:8). Satan first appeared to man in the form of a snake (Gen. 3; II Cor. 11:3).

picture, however, differs slightly. In chapter 16 the seven last plagues occur, and with them the wrath of God ends. The severity and comprehensiveness of the plagues indicate the intensity of God's wrath. In Revelation 16:12, the sixth angel pours his bowl on the river Euphrates. This dries it up to prepare the way for the kings from the east. The judgment following is more comprehensive than the one that followed the sixth trumpet (9:13ff), for then the destruction was limited to one third of mankind. We read of no such limitation here. It is even more obvious here that these war-minded nations are driven by demonic forces, for three foul spirits like frogs appear out of the mouths of the dragon, the beast, and the false prophet.

The demonic forces drive the anti-godly nations to assemble themselves at the place called Harmágedon (often incorrectly referred to as Armageddon). There has been a lot of speculation about this assembly of nations at Harmágedon. The translation of Harmágedon gives us the Mount (Har) of Megiddo (Mágedon). This mountain, just like the Euphrates, functions strategically in the battle between Christ and satan. Barak and Deborah defeated the Canaanite king Jabin and his army there (Judges 5:19), and King Josiah was killed there by Neco, the king of Egypt (II Chron. 35:22ff). At Megiddo, therefore, the Gentiles tried to acquire Canaan, the inheritance of God's people. In the future, apostate powers will launch another large-scale attempt to take away the Church's inheritance. This struggle of the New Testament church can't be geographically located at Megiddo, because the Church is no longer strictly located in Palestine. There is therefore no point in speculating about the time and place of this battle.

It's hard to determine how we *should* picture this struggle, especially since the seven last plagues of

Revelation 16 are described vaguely and symbolically. A comparison with 9:13 does show that this battle is more comprehensive, and that the last phase of history is being described here.

However, here too we are certain that Scripture is not speaking of China as a world power operating in the Middle East during the end times. At one time "the kings of the east" referred to the Gentile powers on the other side of the Euphrates, namely, the Assyrians, the Babylonians, the Medes, and the Persians. But now this term refers to all apostate powers that work to destroy the Church.

11.

Rome on the Road to Revival?

So far we have seen Lindsey paint the rise of three spheres of power playing a role during the end times. The picture is incomplete without the fourth power described in Chapter 8 of his book, which bears the grand title "Rome on the Revival Road." Lindsey claims that the Roman empire of old will be revived shortly before Christ's return. His claim is based on Daniel 7, the vision of the four beasts representing the empires that will successively appear on the world scene. Lindsey says that the first beast is the Babylonian empire, the second is the empire of the Medes and Persians, the third is the Greek empire, and the fourth, described as a terrible monster with iron teeth and nails of brass, is the Roman empire.

This last empire, says Lindsey, will go through two phases. In the first phase it will gain world authority and then disappear until shortly before Christ returns to establish the Kingdom. During the second phase Rome will be a confederacy of ten nations. This can be learned from Daniel 7:20: ". . . and concerning the ten horns that were on its head, and the other horn which came up and before which three of them fell, the horn which had eyes

142

and a mouth that spoke great things, and which seemed greater than its fellows."

Ten nations (ten kings) will come out of Rome, and after them another rather different king will appear. That new king, says Lindsey, is the Antichrist. Whereas people such as Charlemagne, Napoleon and Hitler failed to restore the mighty Roman empire, the Antichrist will succeed. Lindsey says that the beginnings of the prophesied ten-nation confederacy may well lie in the European Common Market and the trend to unify Europe (PE, 83). The next step will be the shift of the West's leadership to Rome in its revived form (PE, 84). At the head of this empire will be the greatest dictator the world has ever known, the Antichrist.

The Spiral Nature of the Book of Daniel

The first question confronting us is whether Lindsey has correctly identified the four beasts. We can quickly dispense with the first beast. It is like a lion and has eagles' wings. It corresponds to the head of gold of Daniel 2, which represents the king of Babylon (Dan. 2:38); therefore we agree with Lindsey that the first beast represents the Babylonian empire. To identify the other three beasts, we must pay attention to the special structure of the book of Daniel. The various visions are closely related to each other, giving the book a strong unity. The visions we are thinking of are the following:

a) the vision of the image with the golden head, etc. (Dan. 2);
b) the vision of the four beasts (Dan. 7);
c) the vision of the ram and the male goat (Dan. 8);
d) the revelation about the seventy weeks (Dan. 9:24-7);
e) the revelation about the "end times."

A comparison of these different parts of the book will produce striking similarities. It will also show that the prophecies about the future become more concentrated as the book progresses. While the writer of the book describes all of history in a nutshell in chapter 2, he gradually adds more details and shortens the historical periods in subsequent sections. And so chapters 10-12 give ample detail for us to determine which kings are referred to in the prophecy.

We might diagram the spiral nature of the book of Daniel as follows:

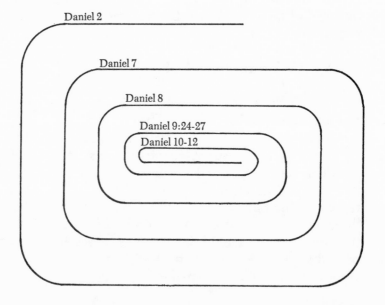

This means that we can determine the identity of the second, third and fourth beasts of Daniel 7 by first looking at the last chapters of the book, where the details are found. You might say that we will be reading this book backwards, or, following the metaphor of the spiral, that we will be looking at it from inside out.

The Seventy Weeks

We will first identify the fourth beast. In an earlier chapter we already said that Daniel 11 describes the period from Daniel's time to the reign of Antiochus Epiphanes. By dividing the chapter into several sections we can be more precise:

a) from Cyrus to the end of Alexander the Great (11:2-4);
b) conflicts between the Ptolemaic dynasty in Egypt (the king of the south) and the Seleucid dynasty in Syria (the king of the north) (11:5-9);
c) the Syrian ruler Antiochus III (11:10-19);
d) his successor Seleucus IV (11:20);
e) Antiochus Epiphanes IV (11:21-45).

Daniel 11:5-20 reveals that the northern kingdom, which had come into being with the help of the southern dynasty, tried to gain the upper hand through a political marriage and through the resulting wars. Antiochus III tried to expand his territory into a world empire, but he failed miserably. Consequently Antiochus Epiphanes found the kingdom in an impoverished and humiliated condition when he became its ruler.

But with this new ruler things took a turn for the better, and the history of Daniel 11 rises to a climax. It is clear that this Syrian king wished to eradicate the true worship of God: "Forces from him shall appear and profane the temple and fortress, and shall take away the continual burnt offering. And they shall set up the abomination that makes desolate" (11:31 RSV). Another verse describes his godless boasting and presumption: "And the king shall do according to his will; he shall exalt himself and magnify himself above every god, and shall speak astonishing things against the God of gods" (vs. 36 RSV).

If we go backwards in the book of Daniel, we will find a passage similar to what we just read about Antiochus Epiphanes in Daniel 11. Look at Daniel 9:26-7:

> And after the sixty-two weeks, an anointed one shall be cut off, and shall have nothing; and the people of the prince who is to come shall destroy the city and the sanctuary. Its end shall come with a flood, and to the end there shall be a war; desolations are decreed. And he shall make a strong covenant with many for one week; and for half of the week he shall cause sacrifice and offering to cease; and upon the wing of abominations shall come one who makes desolate, until the decreed end is poured out on the desolator.

The above passage is part of the prophecy about the seventy weeks (9:24-7). Daniel's reading of Jeremiah's prophecies had made him pray earnestly, and in answer God had sent Gabriel with the prophecy. This happened during the first year of Darius's reign, after the fall of Babylon, and (as Daniel's prayer shows) before Cyrus, the Persian king, allowed the Jews to return to their own country. After the fall of Babylon, Daniel was especially attentive to the amount of time which had passed since Jerusalem had been desolated. From Jeremiah's prophecies he learned that Babylon's rule was to last 70 years, and that God would allow His people to return when 70 years had been completed for Babylon.[1]

---

1. Jeremiah 25:11-12; 29:10. Jeremiah does not prophesy that Judah

Then Daniel understood that there was little time left. As a result, he urgently begged God for deliverance, for return from exile, and for restoration of worship in Jerusalem's temple. God answered him by sending Gabriel with the following message:

> Seventy weeks are marked out for your people and your holy city; then rebellion shall be stopped, sin brought to an end, iniquity expirated, everlasting right ushered in, vision and prophecy sealed, and the Most Holy Place anointed (Dan. 9:24 NEB).

This is a strange way for God to answer Daniel's prayer for the restoration of worship in Jerusalem. Your sins will be forgiven and brought to an end, God tells him. True deliverance will come with the Kingdom of the Son of man.

But a lot will happen before then. Seventy weeks are still marked out for the people and for the city. This number 70 links the message to the prophecies of Jeremiah which had caught Daniel's attention. As a symbol, the number 70 (obviously having the factor 7, the number of fullness) indicates that the time of the Messiah's coming and the establishment of His Kingdom, the time to which Gabriel alludes, will bring complete fulfillment.[2]

---

would be in captivity for exactly 70 years but rather that the nations would serve Babylon for 70 years and that Israel would return (sometime) after those 70 years. The servitude of the nations was evidently calculated from the time of the battle of Carchemish (609 B.C.), where Babylon's universal rule was established with the definitive defeat of the Assyrians. Babylon fell in 539 B.C., exactly 70 years later.

2. In the original, the 70 weeks is actually 70 sevens, that is, a full and complete period of time. We should not think of weeks of years,

When did these 70 weeks begin? Verse 25 tells us: "from the going forth of the word to restore and build Jerusalem." That means that they started from the time that God told Jeremiah about a future full of hope for His people.[3] The first division of the 70 weeks lasts seven weeks, until "the coming of an anointed one, a prince." This must refer to Cyrus, whom the Scriptures call God's "anointed." Cyrus was called to be a world conqueror for the sake of Israel (Is. 45:1,4). Cyrus would issue the edict allowing the Jews to return to Jerusalem to rebuild the city and the temple.

The second division of the 70 weeks will last much longer: 62 weeks. During that time Jerusalem will be completely rebuilt with squares and moat. But the job of rebuilding will not be easy; it will be "a troubled time," a time which the books of Ezra and Nehemiah describe.[4]

In the last of the 70 weeks, an anointed one shall be cut off (vs. 26). There is a difference of opinion as to the identity of this person. He can't be the anointed one of verse 25, because the indefinite article is again used. The King James Version translates the phrase as "Messiah." In our opinion, "an anointed one" refers to the high priest Onias III, who was treacherously murdered in 171 B.C., several years after his brother Jason had acquired his office from Antiochus by bribery (see II Maccabees 4). Un-

---

which would make this a period of 70 x 7 = 490 years. At the end of this period, the era of the Messiah and the new covenant would begin.

3. Another view is that "the going forth of the word" refers to the issuing of an edict by Cyrus, an edict allowing the people to return to Jerusalem. There is more reason to think of God's words to Jeremiah: Gabriel is still explaining Jeremiah's prophecy to Daniel, and the same turn of phrase, the going forth of a word, is used to refer to the speaking of God in verse 23.

4. See especially Ezra 4:1ff; 5:3ff; Neh. 2:10, 19ff; 4:1ff; 6:1ff.

til the time of Antiochus, the dignity of the high priesthood had been preserved, and the high priests had succeeded one another in the line of Eleazar. But at the time of this prophecy's fulfillment, the office had become associated with decadence, corruption, and even murder.

God's judgment comes in the form of "the people of the prince who is to come," who will destroy the city and the sanctuary. Some, thinking that "an anointed one" refers to Christ, see these destructive acts as an allusion to the destruction of the temple by the Romans. But if the anointed one of verse 26 is Onias III, and if we compare Daniel 9:26-7 with 11:31, then this people must be none other than the Syrians under Antiochus Epiphanes, who marched on Jerusalem in 167 B.C., plundered the city, desecrated the temple, and put an end to the offering of sacrifices. (Another argument for this reading is that the prophecies of Daniel keep returning to the time of Antiochus Epiphanes.)

In the next part of the verse, we read that "its end shall come with a flood." The word *its* could also be translated as "his," as the Revised Standard Version acknowledges in a footnote. The end can therefore refer to either the people or the prince mentioned just before this in the same verse. We prefer the translation "his end," thereby letting it refer to Antiochus Epiphanes (of whose death Daniel 11:45 also speaks). By immediately talking about the death of this man, Scripture emphasizes that man's raging comes to nothing, for God puts an end to it when He wills. Antiochus's death shall come by a flood, that is, the flood of God's judgment. Then the prophecy goes on to describe the devastating acts committed by this Syrian ruler.

There will be war until the end of the last "week." This fighting refers to Antiochus's repeated expeditions against Egypt and, more significantly, to his conquest of

Jerusalem and subsequent oppression, and to his last invasion of the glorious land, Israel (11:41).

There is a problem with the translation of the first part of verse 27, which the Revised Standard Version translates: "And he shall make a strong covenant with many for one week." In this version, "he" would have to refer to Christ. A better translation would be: "And he shall make the covenant difficult for many." According to this reading, the covenant refers to God's covenant with Israel, which is also mentioned in 11:28, 30, 32. These verses show that the subject of the sentence in question, the "he," must be Antiochus Epiphanes, for they describe his oppression of those who clung to the covenant, an oppression which made the covenant difficult for them.

That sacrifice and offering will cease (vs. 27) refers not to Christ's abolition of Jewish worship by His death but to the prohibition of Jewish worship by Antiochus Epiphanes. The oppression occurred during the second half of the last "week" (a period of 3 1/2; compare "a time, two times, and a half a time" in 7:25).

The last part of verse 27, about the desolator and the wing of abominations, reminds us of Antiochus's desecration of Jewish worship with the introduction of idolatry in the temple (11:31; 12:11). The "wing" may refer to a protruding part of the temple, possibly the monumental lintel above the main entrance to the hall, on which was probably inscribed the bilingual dedication: "To Zeus Olympios . . . To Baal Shamayim."[5]

According to the last part of the prophecy, the decreed end will be poured out on the desolator, who is, of course, Antiochus Epiphanes. In this prophecy, then, his end coincides with the establishment of the Kingdom

---

5. J. T. Nelis, *Daniel* (Roermond, 1954), p. 109.

of the Messiah, for both occur at the end of the 70 weeks. How is this possible? We are reminded once again that we are dealing with the prophetic perspective, in which events are compressed together. From that perspective the end of the great adversary Antiochus Epiphanes involves the beginning of the Kingdom of the Prince of Peace.

The Fourth Beast

Still reading backwards in the book of Daniel, we come to chapter 8 with its vision of the ram and the male goat. According to the interpretation given to Daniel, the goat represents the king of Greece, or the Greek empire, and the conspicuous horn between the goat's eyes represents the first king. This undoubtedly refers to Alexander the Great, who died shortly after he had established his large dominion. Verse 8 describes him: "Then the he-goat magnified himself exceedingly; but when he was strong, the great horn was broken, and instead of it there came up four conspicuous horns toward the four winds of heaven."

The four new horns refer to the four kingdoms which appeared after Alexander's death. In the vision, a little horn grows out of one of the four horns, and continues to grow greater. This symbol of a king who continues to increase his power represents Antiochus Epiphanes. The horn grows exceedingly great toward the south (Antiochus's expedition against Egypt), toward the east (his campaigns against Armenia and the Parthians), and toward the glorious land (his conquest of Jerusalem).

The activities of Antiochus, the small horn (vs. 10-12, 25), are dreadful. He rises up against the glorious land, Jerusalem. His blasphemous recklessness is so great that he tears some of the stars from the heavens. He exalts

himself in the face of God, the Prince of the host; he
removes the daily offering and destroys God's sanctuary.
This refers to Antiochus's prohibition of Jewish worship.
In its place he institutes a worship of transgression, which
probably refers to the attempt to introduce Greek worship in the temple. Verse 25 reiterates that Antiochus will
rise up against the Prince of princes. Concerning his
death it says: "By no human hand, he shall be broken."
God Himself would destroy him. This prophecy was
fulfilled when Antiochus suddenly died of a mysterious
illness during his campaign against the Parthians.

Many of the details about Antiochus Epiphanes, particularly his vehemence against the people of God and his
humiliating end (Dan. 11:31-5; 9:26-7), correspond to
the details about the little horn in chapter 8.

It is now easy to identify the fourth beast, since there
are various similarities between the male goat of chapter
8 and the fourth beast of chapter 7:

a) Both the male goat and the fourth beast have a little
   horn.
b) The little horn displays a total lack of respect for God.
   Its mouth is full of boasting (7:8, 20); it rises up against
   the Prince of the host and of princes (8:11, 25).
c) The little horn rises up against the people of God. It
   makes war with the saints (7:21), with the glorious land
   and the holy sanctuary, city and temple (8:10-11).
d) The little horn interferes with the worship of God's
   people and introduces pagan worship. It changes the
   times and the law, i.e. the Jewish calendar on which
   the liturgical feasts were based (7:25); it removes the
   daily offering and institutes a sinful kind of worship
   (8:11-12).
e) The little horn dies suddenly; his death is not at the
   hand of a human being (7:11; 8:25).

These similarities clearly demonstrate that the fourth beast of Daniel 7 corresponds to the male goat identified as the king of Greece in 8:21. In other words, the fourth beast represents the Greek empire of Alexander the Great.

Further study will show that the legs of iron in Daniel 2 also correspond to the fourth beast, and that the feet of iron and clay correspond to the Seleucid and Ptolemaic dynasties. About the feet of the image, we read: "They will mix with one another in marriage, but they will not hold together, just as iron does not mix with clay" (2:43 RSV). This corresponds exactly to the situation described in 11:17, namely, that the kings of the north and south vainly try to come to an agreement through a political marriage. From secular history we get further details. The Egyptian king gave his daughter Berenice in marriage to the Syrian king, who then got rid of his first wife. But it didn't work out; the Egyptian king was not able to maintain his advantage. When he died, the Syrian king took back his first wife, who got her revenge by poisoning her husband, killing Berenice and her whole Egyptian royal household, and also the child that had resulted from the marriage.

Daniel 2 gives no details about these events, but Daniel 11 clearly alludes to them. We can conclude that the feet of iron and clay refer to the Ptolemaic and Seleucid dynasties who tried to form a unified political entity but failed. The legs of iron that preceded them must then represent Alexander the Great and must correspond to the fourth beast of Daniel 7.

The Second and the Third Beast

If Alexander is the first king of the fourth kingdom (8:21), then the third beast or kingdom must be the Per-

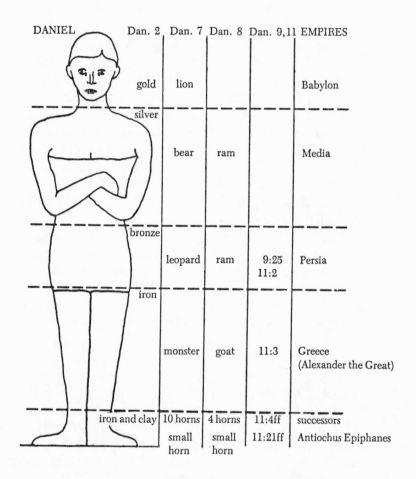

DANIEL	Dan. 2	Dan. 7	Dan. 8	Dan. 9,11	EMPIRES
	gold	lion			Babylon
	silver	bear	ram		Media
	bronze	leopard	ram	9:25 11:2	Persia
	iron	monster	goat	11:3	Greece (Alexander the Great)
	iron and clay	10 horns small horn	4 horns small horn	11:4ff 11:21ff	successors Antiochus Epiphanes

Schematic overview of the book of Daniel

sian empire that was defeated by Alexander in 331. The third beast in Daniel 7 has four heads. This corresponds to 11:2: "Behold, three more kings shall arise in Persia; and a fourth shall be far richer than all of them, and when he has become strong through his riches, he shall stir up all against the kingdom of Greece." There were to be three kings after Cyrus (Daniel's contemporary); then the fourth king must have been Xerxes I (Ahasuerus). His importance lay in his riches, which allowed him to mount a huge campaign against Greece. After him (about 130 years later) arose a "mighty king" who ruled with great dominion (11:3): Alexander the Great.[6]

If the third beast is the Persian empire, then the second beast must be the Median empire. It is sometimes argued that since the Median and Persian empires were unified and concurrent, two consecutive beasts could not represent them. While it is true that the Medes and the Persians enjoyed a certain unity, first one and then the other was predominant.

The vision of the ram in Daniel 8 supports our conclusions. The interpretation given to Daniel says: "As for the ram which you saw with the two horns, these are the kings of Media and Persia" (8:20 RSV). The two horns point to the dual character of the kingdom. But it is also clear that they are not completely concurrent, for the "one [horn] was higher than the other, and the higher one came up last" (vs. 3).

This definitely indicates the successive predominance

---

6. G. C. Aalders disagrees with our explanation of the second and third beasts and the four heads because it implies that Daniel knew only about four Persian kings, whereas there were many more (see *Daniël*, in the "Korte Verklaring" series, p. 139). We would refer the reader to our discussion of the apparent discrepancy on p. 128.

that existed: first the Medes were the leaders, and later the Persians.[7] To the argument that the goat tramples the *one* ram (which we say represents two somewhat successive empires), we reply that in a certain sense the Median empire still lived on within the Persian empire at the time that Alexander destroyed it.

We conclude that the four beasts represent the Babylonian, Median, Persian, and Greek empires. The diagram on p. 154 shows the correspondence between the various visions and the unity behind all that Daniel saw and heard.[8]

The Ten-Nation Confederacy

It should be obvious now that Lindsey's sweeping conclusions about the four beasts of Daniel 7 are totally

7. The Medes were very powerful under Phraortes (674-653 B.C.), who freed them from Assyrian rule. His son and successor Cyaxares (652-584 B.C.) even conquered Nineveh, with the help of the Babylonians. The Medes and the Babylonians divided the Assyrian Empire between them. The last king of the Medes was Astyages (584-550 B.C.). His grandson Cyrus II, king of Anshan, slew Astyages in 550 B.C. and established the Persian empire. In the new empire, the Persians were the rulers, although the Medes did enjoy a privileged position. In 539 the Persians put an end to the power of the neo-Babylonian empire.

8. This interpretation is different from the traditional one, in which the four beasts and the parts of the image represent the Babylonian, Median-Persian, Greek, and Roman empires. The traditional interpretation implies that the numerous small countries found on our world map are the remnants of the Roman empire, represented in the vision by the ten horns and the feet of iron and clay. Out of this situation will come the figure represented by the little horn, a figure who will appear towards the end of world history and who is usually referred to as the Antichrist. But this interpretation fails to take into account the unified and spiral nature of the book of Daniel.

unfounded. When we realize that the fourth beast is not Rome but the Greek empire, we no longer have any basis for claiming that we will shortly witness the second phase of the Roman empire, the ten-nation confederacy, and the "Future Fuehrer" or Antichrist.

Daniel 7 is not about the end times but about political powers during the Old Testament period. It pays special attention to the acts and downfall of Antiochus Epiphanes and to the establishment of the rule of the Son of man, the beginning of the New Testament dispensation.

One might argue that the second and major section of the chapter, beginning with verse 9, certainly seems to be talking about the final judgment and Christ's return on the last day. We read there that the court sits in judgment and that the books are opened (vs. 10). The one like the Son of man comes with the clouds of heaven (vs. 13). Is this not the final judgment and Christ's return in glory? Not necessarily. Let's take a closer look.

While Daniel continues to be stunned by the "great things" coming from the mouth of the fourth beast's little horn, another scene unfolds before his eyes. He sees the heavenly court, with the Ancient of Days presiding. The books containing the indictments are opened, the sentences are pronounced, and the fourth beast is killed on account of the blasphemies uttered by its little horn. The power of the other beasts is also removed. This corresponds to the stone's simultaneous destruction of all the parts of the image in Daniel 2.

Then Daniel sees the Son of man coming with the clouds of heaven, and to Him is given everlasting dominion (7:13-14). This prophecy is not primarily about Christ's return but about His ascension to the throne. The end of the rule of Antiochus Epiphanes ushered in the everlasting rule of Christ, which began when He conquered death. Easter demanded the ascension: the Son of man, to whom all authority in heaven and on earth was given (Matt. 28:18), had to ascend to His heavenly throne.

The coming of the Son of man with the clouds of heaven in Daniel 7 does not refer to Christ's return at the end of history. That He comes "with the clouds" means that His power and glory will be evident when He comes to the throne of God as the legitimate heir to David's royal line.

The New Testament amplifies the revelation of God found in Daniel 7:13. The gospels and the book of Revelation repeat this prophecy, using slightly different wordings.[9] When the high priest asks Jesus during His trial whether He is the Christ, the Son of God, He answers affirmatively and quotes Daniel 7:13 to show the true nature of His authority: "But I tell you, hereafter you will see the Son of man seated at the right hand of Power, and coming on the clouds of heaven" (Matt. 26:64 RSV).

This answer combines two passages of Scripture, Daniel 7:13 and Psalm 110:1.[10] The latter verse describes the accession to the throne by David's lord: "The Lord says to my lord: 'Sit at my right hand, till I make your enemies your footstool.' " Only when Christ connected these two passages did the members of the high tribunal understand that He was the Messiah, the Priest-King of Psalm 110 who would sit at God's right hand and the

---

9. The following variations exist: *with* the clouds (Mark 14:62; Rev. 1:7); *on* the clouds (Matt. 24:30; 26:64); *in* clouds, *in* a cloud (Mark 13:26; Luke 21:27). A comparison of these passages show that these prepositions are used interchangeably.

10. See also the parallel passages: Mark 14:62 and Luke 22:69. In the latter passage Jesus quotes only from Psalm 110.

King of Daniel 7 who would be inaugurated to rule forever from the throne of heaven.

This is what Christ said about Himself while He was on trial before the Sanhedrin, knowing all the while what they were going to do to Him. The path of the Priest-King led to the throne of heaven only by way of the cross. "Hereafter you will see the Son of man . . . ." The word *hereafter* refers exclusively to neither Christ's appearance on the last day nor to the day of Easter. Rather, there is a continuous process at work, one that began with the resurrection and will be culminated on the last day. In this way Christ brought the prophecy of Daniel to bear on His coming glorification and accession to the throne and His return in glory (see Matt. 24:30; Rev. 1:7), which will consummate His ascension to the throne.

There is really no point in identifying the ten horns of the beast. The number 10 as such is used to indicate the totality of kings who would issue from the Greek empire. These kings are the kings of the four Diadochian kingdoms, in particular the many Seleucid kings who would rule before Antiochus Epiphanes appeared on the scene. After the ten kings "another shall arise . . . different from the former ones, and shall put down three kings" (7:24 RSV). This refers to Antiochus, who would craftily push aside other claimants to the throne to acquire power (11:21).

The saints of the Most High will be delivered into his power "for a time, two times, and half a time" (7:25). This period of 3 1/2 is related to 9:27, which speaks about the cessation of sacrifice and offering "for half of the week." At stake here is a development that is prematurely ended at its halfway point. The prophecy here foresees how Antiochus's severe persecution of God's people is interrupted (by his death) before he will be able to achieve his goal of wiping out the worship of God.

This prophecy was a comfort to the Jews during the time of persecution. It is also a comfort to the New Testament church, which has been persecuted by her enemies since Pentecost. The promise given to Daniel is sure, because Jesus Christ rules in heaven, guiding history towards the day of His glorious return on the clouds of heaven.

12

A Future Fuehrer?

Hal Lindsey devotes many pages to the "Great Dictator" or "Future Fuehrer" (his terms for the Antichrist that he finds in the Scriptures). He says that the Bible gives a "perfect biographical sketch" of this future world leader (PE, 92), the details being in the vision of the beast coming out of the sea (Rev. 13). Lindsey says this beast is the Antichrist, the one who will be the dictator of the revived Roman empire.

This revived Roman empire comes from Daniel 7 and the fourth beast. Lindsey says that ten kings will come out of the culture of the first Roman empire before the appearance of a different king, one who will put himself at the head of the ten-nation confederacy. This will be the dictatorial Antichrist. Seven of the kings or leaders will willingly give their allegiance, but three will not, and these he will overthrow (PE, 94). Lindsey finds this in Revelation 13:1; for him the ten horns of the beast refer to the ten nations of the confederacy, and its seven heads are the seven leaders who form a coalition with the Antichrist.

161

The beast that comes out of the sea has the characteristics of the first three beasts of Daniel 7: it was like a
leopard, its feet were like a bear's feet, and its mouth was
like a lion's mouth. Lindsey concludes that the Antichrist
will be quick to conquer like the leopard and the Greek
empire, strong and powerful like the bear and the
Median-Persian empire, and proud and self-assured like
the lion and the Babylonian empire (PE, 94-5).

Lindsey makes a great deal of the beast's mortal
wound (Rev. 13:3). He says that the Great Dictator will
be critically wounded at a time when he is not yet known
as a great leader. But he will survive his wounds to
become a hero. The whole world will follow him (PE,
97).

The 42 months mentioned in Revelation 13:5 tell
Lindsey that the Future Fuehrer will be given authority
to carry out his godless actions for 3 1/2 years. These years
of his rule will immediately precede Christ's personal
return to earth. The beast, according to 13:7, opens its
mouth to blaspheme God's name and dwelling, and those
who dwell in heaven. Lindsey understands the latter to
be those who were taken up before the Tribulation to live
in heaven during the 3 1/2 years of the Antichrist's
regime.

Scripture goes on to say that the beast "was allowed
to make war on the saints and to conquer them" (13:7
RSV). Here Lindsey finds it logical to ask, "How is he
going to make war with the saints when they are gone
from the earth?" (PE, 99). Lindsey, of course, has an answer ready. After the Christians are gone, God will reveal
Himself in a special way to 144,000 physical, literal Jews,
who will then believe in Christ with a vengeance. Their
furious evangelism will produce the greatest number of
converts in all history. In fact, they will be innumerable,
according to Revelation 7:9-14. Against these converts

the Antichrist will unleash a total persecution. He will be the absolute dictator of the whole world: "And authority was given it over every tribe and people and tongue and nation" (Rev. 13:7).

The Identity of the Beast

The reader probably already doubts that Revelation 13 actually gives a biographical description of "the Antichrist" of the end times. Let's take a closer look at the beast that John saw rising out of the sea of nations. Its ten horns and seven heads give it a striking resemblance to the dragon (satan) of Revelation 12:3. To the beast "the dragon gave his power and his throne and great authority" (vs. 2). This means that though the beast resembles satan, it can't be identified with satan. When the beast is given satan's power, it becomes his instrument, carrying out his will.

The vision of Revelation 13 features the four beasts of Daniel 7 in the opposite order of their appearance to Daniel. In the first verse we are reminded of the dreadful fourth beast by the ten horns of the beast out of the sea. In the second verse the beast is compared to the leopard, the bear and the lion. But instead of four separate beasts, John sees one beast with the characteristics of the Greek, Persian, Median, and Babylonian empires. The beast out of the sea therefore embodies the various godless forces of the latter part of the Old Testament period. It represents godless, anti-Christian state power.

Not only that, it represents a *concentration* of this force, for Revelation 13 begins with a reference to the fourth beast. It may seem perfectly natural for John to see first the horns of a beast that is rising out of the sea. However, there is more at stake here: Revelation 13 is beginning where Daniel 7 left off. Daniel's vision ended with the fourth and most dreadful beast, who represented the climax of the violence of the godless state power that occurred at the hand of Antiochus Epiphanes. This means that the beast out of the sea represents the epitome of godless state power.

We must see the beast, therefore, not as a person but as a force or power, just as the four beasts in Daniel's vision represented world powers. In the interpretation of Daniel's dream, we do read about "four kings who shall arise out of the earth," but this refers to four empires.[1]

Just as there was no point in identifying the ten horns of Daniel's fourth beast, so there is no point in identifying the ten horns of the beast from the sea. The important thing is that the number 10 indicates a fullness of power. We reject Lindsey's claim that the beast's seven heads represent seven leaders who form a coalition with the Antichrist. His claim is based on an incorrect interpretation of Daniel 7:24, which speaks about a king who will appear after ten kings and will put down three kings. That king, as we have seen, refers to Antiochus Epiphanes—not to a "Future Fuehrer." It is arbitrary to

---

1. Many people claim that the beasts refer to specific persons. It is true that the Greek empire could be identified with Alexander the Great (see Dan. 11:3). It is also true that Daniel says to King Nebuchadnezzar, "You are the head of gold" (2:37-8). Yet the book of Daniel does speak about another king before the disappearance of the renewed Babylonian empire, namely, Belshazzar, who temporarily replaced King Nabonidus. Daniel 2:39 continues with "After you shall arise another kingdom . . . ." The Persian empire did begin with Cyrus, but Daniel speaks of three kings after him (11:2). Finally, it does say that the "four great beasts are four kings who shall arise out of the earth" (7:17), but if these kings are persons, then, to be consistent, the fourth king must also be a person, something which no one ever concludes.

say that the seven heads are seven kings who form a coalition with the Antichrist.

There is no point in trying to identify the seven heads, for a seven-headed monster was a common image of antiquity. For example, excavations in Ugarit uncovered the image of a monster with seven heads, each on top of another, of which three looked alive. The seven-headed beast that John saw represented the godless state power heaping sin upon sin.

We reject the rather common interpretation in which the seven heads refer to seven successive kingdoms. In this view the mortal wound that the beast receives becomes the deadly blow that ended the Roman empire. The revival of the beast then refers to the revival of godless state power.[2] We object to this interpretation on two grounds. First, as we have seen, it is futile to try to identify the seven heads. Second, this interpretation is incorrect in its determination of the time period in which

---

2. S. Greijdanus sees the seven heads as "successive world empires that replaced each other in the course of the centuries." The heads refer to the ancient Babylonian, Egyptian, Assyrian, Chaldean-Babylonian, Median-Persian, Greek, and Roman empires. The eighth king (17:9,11) refers to the Antichrist, who, with his great world power, will be the last incarnation of the beast out of the sea. The deadly wound refers to the downfall of Roman world rule. The healing of the wound refers to the rise of papal power and the rise of the godless world rule which is still coming (*Openbaring*, in the "Korte Verklaring" series, p. 204).

In Benne Holwerda's scheme, the Egyptian empire is omitted and the Roman empire is the sixth head. It receives a deadly blow from which it never recovered. That one empire was replaced by numerous countries. The attempts to reunify the world (Louis XIV, Napoleon, Hitler) have failed. But today we begin to see the seventh head in the growth of world unity. It won't be long before we see the whole beast, the last appearance of the Antichrist as the eighth world emperor (*Populair Wetenschappelijke Bijdragen*, Goes, 1962, pp. 163ff).

the beast carries on its activities. Revelation says that the beast has power for 42 months. As we saw in Chapters 3 and 5, these 42 months in Revelation indicate the whole New Testament period of history. They do not refer to the Old Testament period of world empires, nor exclusively to a block of time at the end of world history.

The beast oppresses the church for 42 months, that is, from the time of Christ's ascension to heaven (referred to in Revelation 12:5) to His return. This period is a fearful one for the Church. Although Christ is already King (12:10), Scripture still says, "But woe to you, O earth and sea, for the devil has come down to you in great wrath, because he knows that his time is short!" (12:12). It is during this time that the devil gives his power and throne to the beast, the godless state power.

Forty-two months are equal to 3 1/2 years. This makes us think of the time, two times, and half a time that Antiochus Epiphanes would oppress the Old Testament church (Dan. 7:25). This period foreshadowed the constant persecution of the New Testament period. As Scripture says, "Indeed all who desire to live a godly life in Christ Jesus will be persecuted" (II Tim. 3:12). According to the vision of Revelation 13, the persecution of the church will primarily originate with the godless state power. It began with the Roman emperors' persecution of the Christians and will continue to the end of the New Testament dispensation. The end of the ages is already upon us!

One of the beast's heads seems to have a mortal wound. This makes us think of the three lifeless heads of the seven-headed figure found in Ugarit. The one head that we are talking about, however, was not dead but mortally wounded. Nobody would have expected it to mend, but it miraculously heals. This does not refer, as Lindsey says, to a man, the Antichrist who manages to

pass by death's door. It refers to what happens to the
godless state power. It's pointless to speculate which of
the seven heads or which kingdom is injured. We have to
keep in mind the total picture of the beast being given a
mortal injury. The fatal stab was driven home with
Christ's victory over death and His accession to the
heavenly throne (see John 12:32; 14:30; 16:11; Col. 2:15;
Rev. 12:9; see also our discussion of Rev. 20:1-10 in
Chapter 4).

The beast that John sees coming out of the sea has
already been wounded. This prophetic injury was
fulfilled in the inroads the gospel made immediately after
Christ's ascension. Even with the shadow of Rome
hanging everywhere, the gospel of Christ was powerfully
triumphant, being preached and received throughout the
known world of that time. That this was possible is really
quite unbelievable. But it was, through Christ's victory
over the dragon. On Golgotha He had dealt a deadly
blow to the old snake who controlled and tempted the
nations. Then Christ entered heaven in royal triumph.
That is why the gospel could march victoriously through
the world and why the impressive beast with the ten
horns and seven heads on John's television screen was
mutilated. It had been fatally wounded, and to all ap-
pearances it was going to die.

The miracle occurs. The beast recovers. It is
significant that the recovery does occur within the vision.
By this recovery we should understand that the godless
state power quickly regained the offensive. The Roman
empire could only tolerate one kind of worship, the worship of the emperor; it began to persecute the Christians.

The whole earth follows the beast with wonder, says
John. They worship the dragon and the beast. As the
masses kneel before the godless forces, they cry, "Who is
like the beast, and who can fight against it?" This

describes the situation in which the church finds herself during the New Testament dispensation. She is surrounded by the godless state power that entices millions of people to its worship. She is often hard pressed to find evidence that Christ has been and is victorious.

The beast is given a mouth that utters haughty and blasphemous words. This reminds us of the "little horn" of Daniel 7:25, who spoke against the Most High and wore out His saints. This of course was Antiochus Epiphanes, whose blasphemy against God and persecution of God's people typified the actions of the godless state power of the New Testament dispensation. This force is at war with God and His saints. Just as Christ rules over the whole world and gathers His Church everywhere, so the beast makes his attacks everywhere. It was given authority over every tribe and people and tongue and nation (13:7).

"Those Who Dwell in Heaven"

The preceding discussion has made it clear that Revelation 13 gives no basis for Lindsey's view that the beast out of the sea is a personal Antichrist who will oppress the whole world just before Christ's return. Several details still demand closer attention.

In connection with the statement in Revelation 13:6 that the beast will blaspheme God's name, His dwelling, and those who dwell in heaven, Lindsey remarks:

> This is interesting. Why would he "blaspheme" or "bad-mouth" those who will dwell in heaven? And who are the ones who dwell in heaven; why would he even bother with them? You and I are the ones who are going to dwell in heaven, if we are true believers in Jesus Christ (PE, 99).

We will be in heaven because Lindsey believes that the Christians will have been taken up in the Rapture: "We believe that Christians will not be around to watch the debacle brought about by the cruelest dictator of all time" (p. 102).

But that is not Scriptural. The Bible says that God's children go to heaven when they die, and not that they are taken up just before the Tribulation, after which the onus would be on Israel, the 144,000 Jewish Billy Grahams, to make the many converts against whom persecution will rage. Those in heaven are the ones who are with God, surrounded by His glory; they enjoy the bliss of heaven. It includes the angels, God's servants, who stand before His face.

Why does the beast blaspheme against them? Because he is consumed by a venomous hatred against God. This hatred is evident today in the Communist forces of Russia and China, who deny the very existence of God and heaven, and whose propaganda claims that religion is nothing more than the "opiate of the people."

Who are the saints that the beast defeats? (13:7). According to the Scriptures, the New Testament believers on earth are saints. Here again Revelation 13 links itself to Daniel's prophecy: "As I looked, this horn made war with the saints, and prevailed over them" (Dan. 7:21 RSV). Just as Antiochus Epiphanes fought with the Old Testament saints, so the godless state power fights against the New Testament saints. These saints are not just converted Jews, for the New Testament calls Christians from any and all nations "saints." The saints are those who have been redeemed out of all generations.

The Beast out of the Earth

Another detail demanding our attention is Lindsey's

interpretation of the beast out of the earth. Concerning this beast who represents false prophecy, Revelation 13:14 says, "And by the signs which it is allowed to work in the presence of the beast, it deceives those who dwell on earth, bidding them make an image for the beast which was wounded by the sword and yet lived." Lindsey infers that this beast is a false prophet who will collaborate with the Roman Dictator. The latter will have a statue made of himself, and the False Prophet will entice people to worship this idol.

Lindsey says, "You do not make an idol of an empire. You make an idol of a person" (p. 97). That's not true. Look at what Nebuchadnezzar did. In the plain of Dura he set up a golden image, and all the dignitaries were assembled for the dedication ceremony, to fall down and worship the image. This was an idol, an image of the power and greatness of the Babylonian empire. It was an idolization of the state power of Babylon. The glory of Babylon may have been concentrated in the person of Nebuchadnezzar, but the image was primarily the symbol of the mighty world empire of Babylon.

The beast out of the earth, i.e. false prophecy, deceives the people into making an image of the beast out of the sea. In other words, he ensures that humanity pays homage to the godless state power as if it were a god. This beast also makes sure that everyone receives a mark on his forehead or on his right hand; without it no one may buy or sell.

We should not defer these events to the future, nor should we transform the actors into a gruesome Fuehrer and his accomplice the False Prophet. Rather, they refer to the present dispensation, which began when Christ died, rose and ascended into heaven. Ever since that time, the two beasts, godless state power and false prophecy, have collaborated in tempting mankind to worship the former and to boycott genuine believers.

In certain periods of history, their actions appear in sharper relief than in other periods. We know their activity will intensify as the day of Christ's return approaches. Today we see their influence increasing in the way that television, radio and the press are willing to further the ends of neo-Marxist propaganda. People are gradually softened; they are made ready and willing to worship the beast of Communism. It is clear that Communism is rapidly gaining favor and increasing its international power. Everywhere godless state power tightens its grip on the masses, and soon the boycott of all who refuse to worship may be upon us.

The Man of Lawlessness

In connection with the would-be Antichrist, Lindsey also refers to Paul's remarks in II Thessalonians 2 about the man of lawlessness "who opposes and exalts himself against every so-called god or object of worship, so that he takes his seat in the temple of God, proclaiming himself to be God" (vs. 4). According to Lindsey, this means that the Antichrist will proclaim himself God. He will establish himself in the temple of God, which can only be found on Mount Moriah in Jerusalem, where the Dome of the Rock and other Moslem shrines now stand. Paul says that the man of lawlessness is not yet revealed because there is one "who now restrains" (vs. 7); that restrainer, according to Lindsey, is "the restraining power of the Spirit of God, within believing Christians." Only after these Christians are taken up will the Antichrist be able to establish himself and exert his power and might throughout the world (PE, 98).

What Paul says in this chapter certainly does raise some questions. Is he talking about a personal Antichrist, one who appears at the end of history? What is meant by "the temple of God"? To begin with, we should notice that in verse 4, Paul is echoing Daniel 11:36: "And the king shall do according to his will; he shall exalt himself and magnify himself above every god, and shall speak astonishing things against the God of gods." We have seen that this refers to the attitude and actions of Antiochus Epiphanes. Paul thinks of him in connection with the man of lawlessness. He calls the latter "the son of perdition," meaning that he, just like Antiochus Epiphanes, will perish in spite of his presumption and boasting.

The King James Version translates II Thessalonians 2:2 as follows: "That ye be not soon shaken in mind, or be troubled . . . as that the day of Christ is at hand." According to a common interpretation, Paul is here warning his audience that Christ will not return as shortly as some would have them believe, that a lot of things will still take place before His return. We don't agree with this interpretation. If so many places in the New Testament say that the day of the Lord is at hand,[3] how can Paul here be saying that it is still a long way off?

The phrase "at hand" in verse 2 ("as that the day of Christ is at hand") indicates something that is presently occurring. Paul is not saying, "Don't believe that the day of the Lord is coming soon," but rather, "Don't think that what you now see is the day of the Lord."

We might translate verses 1-3a as follows: "We ask you brothers, with an eye to the appearance of the Lord Jesus and our gathering together to meet Him (so that you will not be easily disturbed or dissuaded by an oracular

---

3. Romans 13:12; Philippians 4:5; James 5:8; I Peter 4:7. According to I Corinthians 7:29, the time has grown "very short" (literally: compressed). Christ testifies that He is coming soon (Rev. 3:11; 22:7, 12, 20).

utterance or explanation or a letter, as if people could appeal to us for the message that the day of the Lord has come)—we ask you not to let anyone deceive you in any way, because first there will be a falling away . . . ."

This translation makes it clear that Paul is warning the congregation at Thessalonica that they should not be prematurely persuaded that the day of the Lord has arrived. Before that day comes, they will witness a falling away and the appearance of the man of lawlessness. What is Paul's concern? That when the man of lawlessness appears, many will think they are witnessing the beginning of the new era they have been expecting. They will even appeal to the Scriptures (Paul's letters) in order to welcome the man of lawlessness, saying "This is what we have been waiting for!"

The man of lawlessness will take his seat in the temple of God. This does not mean the temple in Jerusalem, because in New Testament terms the temple of God is the body of believers in Christ.[4] This prophecy was pregnant with meaning for the people at the time of the Reformation. In Calvin's opinion, Paul's remarks about the man of lawlessness who took his seat in the temple could only refer to the papacy.[5] It was said that the papacy was trying to drive the true God out of the church, put itself in His place, and exalt itself through sacrilege. This conviction was common among the Calvinists, and it per-

---

4. See I Corinthians 3:16-17; II Corinthians 6:16; Ephesians 2:21. Others disagree. J. van Bruggen says the temple in Jerusalem is meant, and points to the Roman emperor Caligula's demand that his statue be put in the temple of Jerusalem in A.D. 39. He died before his demand was met, however. Lindsey, of course, also looks to the temple in Jerusalem, which he says will be rebuilt before Christ's return. We fail to find any Scriptural basis for this.

5. *The Institutes of the Christian Religion*, IV, 2, 12.

sisted a long time.[6] Our predecessors in the faith therefore saw the man of lawlessness within their time, within the church, and did not defer his appearance to some nebulous "end time."

What does Paul mean by the restraining power or person in verses 6 and 8? Different opinions exist. People used to say that the Roman empire was doing the restraining, and that the emperor, as representative of that empire, was the restrainer. Another opinion, held by some of the church fathers and by Calvin, was that the man of lawlessness was restrained by the fact that the gospel had not yet been preached to all nations. Only when that was done could the end come.

In our opinion we need to take a different tack. We should see that whereas verse 6 talks about that which restrains Jesus Christ, verse 7 talks about what restrains the lawless one. In this way the passage is no longer a riddle, and it becomes easy to paraphrase Paul's words: "By this time you know what is restraining Jesus Christ. Didn't I tell you? First the rebellion must come. Its absence restrains Christ. Be on your guard against the rebellion and its man of lawlessness. Be careful that you don't welcome this man's day as if it were the day of the Lord. For even though the man of lawlessness has not yet appeared, the mystery of lawlessness is already at work. That lawlessness will be revealed in history according to God's plan. Just be ready for the time when he who restrains the lawless one is removed."

---

6. In the preface to the Canons of Dort, we read that "by God's mighty hand the Church in these countries has been delivered from the tyranny of the Roman Antichrist and the dreadful idolatry of the papacy." A. Hellenbroek (1658-1731) wrote that "everything predicted about the Antichrist in II Thessalonians 2:1-11 is fulfilled in the Roman pope."

Who is it that restrains the lawless one? Hal Lindsey
says that it is the power of the Spirit of God within
believing Christians. Therefore the taking up of the
Christians during the Rapture will give the man of
lawlessness free rein. We reject this view because the idea
of the Rapture is unscriptural and because the man of
lawlessness should not be seen as a personality of the end
times.

It's more correct to think of the restrainer as a
divinely ordained supernatural power, such as a mighty
angel. We come to this conclusion by reading II
Thessalonians 2 together with Daniel 10 and 11, two
chapters which form a unity. In chapter 10, before the
rule of Antiochus Epiphanes, a mighty angel wrestles
with a demon in order to check the Persian and Greek
violence and so to protect God's people. This means that
a struggle in the spiritual world lies behind the struggles
on earth. With this in mind, we should read about the
struggle of satan against God in II Thessalonians 2: it is a
mighty angel who checks the coming of the lawless one
and thereby restrains the ultimate revelation of satan's
power.

Paul was writing in A.D. 51. Since then "the
rebellion" has come, and with it the man of lawlessness.
Think of how the Reformers saw the man of lawlessness
and the Antichrist in the papacy. However, it is not
correct to identify the man of lawlessness with the Antichrist. Notice that Paul makes no mention of the Antichrist. Rather, it is the apostle John who talks about the
Antichrist. While he says that "many antichrists have
come" (I John 2:18), these can't be seen as precursors of
the Antichrist because "the Antichrist" had already come
in John's days: "Who is the liar but he who denies that
Jesus is the Christ? This is the antichrist, he who denies
the Father and the Son" (I John 2:22). In verse 7 of II

John he says, "Such a one is the deceiver and the antichrist," meaning one who denies the coming of Christ in the flesh. For John, therefore, the Antichrist is concentrated in the lie, in the false doctrine that was appearing in the church. The Antichrist comes from within the (apostate) church.

The man of lawlessness, like Antiochus Epiphanes, comes from outside the church, ensconces himself within it, and acquires the power needed to dethrone God. The Antichrist and the man of lawlessness are in fact quite similar; they can cooperate in propagating their apostate theology. But the lawless one enters the church from without, while the Antichrist comes from within the church.

The Antichrist is not a military tyrant but someone who deceptively pushes false doctrine. The "beast out of the earth" in Revelation 13 can't be the Antichrist, because the prophecy relates this beast to godless state power; this power is "anti-Christ" but is not the Antichrist.

Although we might disagree with the Reformers' identification of the two figures or powers, we should give them credit for recognizing, in their specific situation, what Paul could only vaguely refer to as the "mystery" of lawlessness. For us as church today, it is also of prime importance to recognize the man of lawlessness. To get a better idea of what we are looking for, we should once more look at II Thessalonians 2 in conjunction with Daniel 11.

At the time with which Daniel 11 concerns itself, satan's struggle against Christ was concentrating itself in Antiochus's attempt to Hellenize the Jewish religion. That is to say, the Jewish religion was to become part of a large-scale process of syncretism, in which all kinds of religions would be forged into one world religion.

Hellenism was poised to deliver a deadly blow to the Jewish religion, the religion of revelation:

> It replaced redemption through the revelation from above by the seed of the woman with the ascent of man from below towards god by means of the mystery worship of the Greek gods. In place of the adoration of the living God made without human hands, it put the worship of idols who were the incarnation of the pagan Greek gods, an incarnation not miraculously wrought from above but produced by human hands.[7]

We should keep in mind that this danger threatened the Jewish church on account of her own apostasy. Daniel 8:23 says that the oppressive king will arise "when the transgressors have reached their full measure," that is, when many Jews have fallen away from true worship. The Greek religion, the modernism of that day, had a tremendous attraction for Israel. But when apostasy reached its height, God intervened and raised up Antiochus Epiphanes, a forerunner of the man of lawlessness.

The church today has eased away from faithful adherence to God's Word, and consequently we see the man of lawlessness, in the form of a godless force[8] sneaking into the church. It is the spirit of the times, rather than God's Word, that sets the tone in modern theology; the world determines the church's beliefs. If

---

7. R. H. Bremmer, *Man contra moker*, pp. 67-8.
8. The man of lawlessness does not necessarily refer to a person. J. Jeremias points out that there is a Semitic way of speaking by which one refers to something abstract by way of a possessive construction (see *TWB*, I, p. 365). We do the same thing ourselves when we speak of "the man of the twentieth century."

this trend is allowed to continue, it will eradicate the Christian faith.

People today want to see Christianity as a typically human concern. There is no longer room for an active God who, from without, reveals Himself within and to this world. Man replaces God. This is a denial of the Christian faith. Man decides what he will believe: only what opens the future or gives freedom to mankind is termed a Christian truth.

The tragedy is that people appeal to the Scriptures for these godless theories. Let us take note of Paul's warning of long ago: we must not welcome the day of man as the day of the Lord. We must discern the appearance of apostasy (the man of lawlessness), so that we will remain steadfast in our expectation of the One who by His glorious appearance will eliminate the lawless one.

13

Revelation 17, the Woman and Babylon

Revelation 17

Now we are coming to some of the most important pieces of the prophetic puzzle which are shown in the Scriptures. In Revelation 17 the apostle John has a vision which shows the future and precisely what is going to happen on earth the last seven years before Christ returns. In Revelation 17 John is given one of the most important prophecies for us to understand because he is exposing a one-world religious system which will bring all false religions together in one unit. Through this system Satan's Antichrist will take over the world—and he is going to do it first with Rome as home base and then from Jerusalem (PE, 110-11).

This quotation comes from the chapter "Revival of Mystery Babylon," in which Lindsey discusses the vision of the woman on the scarlet beast. According to Lindsey, the woman represents a world religion that will hold sway before the return of Christ. He calls it the "mystery religion of Babylon" (PE, 112).

179

How does Lindsey arrive at this? John says of the woman that "on her forehead was written a name of mystery: 'Babylon' " (Rev. 17:5). For Lindsey these words refer to the ancient religion of Babylon. Its basis was astrology. From the Genesis account of the building of the tower of Babel, Lindsey learns that astrology had its origins in Babylon. "Then they said, 'Come, let us build ourselves a city, and a tower with its top in the heavens' " (Gen. 11:4). Lindsey says that the word *tower* can refer to a ziggurat, the observatory from which priests in ancient times observed the stars. By charting them, the priests predicted the future.

Therefore the woman represents the mystery religion of Babylon which will soon rise to predominance: "We believe that the joining of churches in the present ecumenical movement, combined with this amazing rejuvination of star-worship, mind-expansion, and witchcraft, is preparing the world in every way for the establishment of a great religious system, one which will influence the Antichrist" (PE, 104-5). The beast on which the woman rides is the Antichrist, the Future Fuehrer, and its ten horns refer to the revived Roman empire. The riding of the beast shows that the woman, or the religion, controls him.

Lindsey gets a lot of information from Revelation 17:9-10:

> This calls for a mind with wisdom: the seven heads are seven mountains on which the woman is seated; they are also seven kings, five of whom have fallen, one is, the other has not yet come, and when he comes he must remain only a little while.

Lindsey relates the "five kings" to five former kingdoms over which the mystery religion of Babylon exerted authority: the Chaldean, Egyptian, neo-Babylonian,

Median-Persian, and Greek world kingdoms. The kingdom that still is is the Roman empire, which existed when the apostle John was writing. The mystery religion of Babylon exerted great influence in the Roman empire, according to Lindsey. The seventh king, who has not yet come, is the revived Roman empire. The Antichrist will come up out of the culture of the ancient Roman empire. After establishing himself as head of the ten-nation confederacy, he will transform it into an eighth world power, the revived Roman empire. Lindsey already sees signs of its coming: "We believe that we are seeing, with all of the other signs, the revival of Mystery, Babylon—not just in astrology, but also in spiritism, a return to the supernatural, and in drugs" (PE, 113).

The whore of Revelation 17 not only represents a religious system but also a city. Lindsey has no doubt that Rome is meant by the seven hills on which the woman sits (or rules). For a while the religious system will form a coalition with the political system in Rome. Then the Great Dictator will begin to hate the religious system, because he no longer wants to be its puppet. The destruction of the religious system will take place in two phases: first the dictator will destroy the religious system, and then the city of Rome will suddenly be destroyed.

The Mystery Religion of Babylon

Lindsey finds an indication of the Babylonian mystery religion in the story of the tower of Babel. Though astronomy was important to the Babylonians and Babylon did boast of a famous towering ziggurat, it is not correct to identify the tower of Genesis 11 as a ziggurat.[1]

---

1. The Hebrew word that is translated as "tower" here often occurs

According to the Biblical account, the builders were interested in something much different than astronomy. They wanted a tall tower that would be visible everywhere, so that they would always be able to find it back and not be scattered across the earth. They were looking for strength in unity, a strength that was directed against God: they wanted to make a name for *themselves*.

On the harlot's forehead was written the name *mystery*, meaning the great Babylon, the mother of harlots and of earth's abominations. The harlot was drunk with the blood of the saints and the martyrs of Jesus (17:5-6). She represents the apostate church,[2] otherwise known as the great Babylon. The name is a mystery in the sense that it is not a geographical reference but a characterization of the true nature of the woman.[3] She does not represent the city of God but the city where mankind assembles to rebel against God. As a dolled-up harlot, she is the counterpart of the bride of Christ that

---

in Scripture in the sense of watchtower, bulwark, or defense (see II Chron. 26:9-10, 15; 32:5; II Kings 17:9; Judges 9:51-2; Ps. 49:12; 61:3; Is. 30:25; Ezek. 26:9). A. van Selms says that this word refers to a bulwark, either as part of the city wall or as an independent structure. He says that the identification of the tower in Genesis 11 with a ziggurat is not justified. In his opinion, the idea of the tower was to build a fortified city as the center of humanity, and especially for the people to make a name for themselves, that is, to make a monument to themselves. By contrast, in Psalm 48 the wall and ramparts of Jerusalem are seen as a monument to the glory of God.

2. See. Benne Holwerda, "De 'hoer' in Openbaring 17-19," in *Populaire Wetenschappelijke Bijdragen*, pp. 127ff.

3. Compare the use of "mystery" in several other passages in Revelation (1:20; 10:7). Greijdanus writes that the word *musterion* (mystery, secret), indicates that this is no ordinary given name but a name with a symbolic meaning (compare vs. 7) that must be understood in a spiritual, metaphorical sense (*Kommentaar N.T.*, p. 341).

John saw in Revelation 12. She may call herself "the church," but, John says, she is in fact "Babylon."

Lindsey's fantasy about the mystery religion of Babylon comes from his incorrect interpretation of Genesis 11:4 and of the word *mystery* in Revelation 17. We, too, are concerned about the revival of astrology and black magic and the growing enslavement to drugs. But we don't find this trend predicted by Revelation 17.

The Woman on the Scarlet Beast

The harlot is also a "great city which has dominion over the kings of the earth" (17:18). Lindsey says that the city refers to Rome because the woman sits (or rules) on seven hills. From there Lindsey goes on to talk about a religious system that will rule in Rome. However, the woman does not sit on seven hills according to 17:9 but on seven mountains, which are not to be found in Rome.[4]

Besides, the number 7 here should be viewed in a different light. It is related to the seven heads of the beast. We have already seen that a seven-headed beast was a common theme of ancient images. The seven heads are seven mountains (17:9). Seven mountains was another common theme. On ancient Eastern seals one repeatedly finds a god depicted on a throne formed by mountains heaped on top of one another. The seven mountains therefore do not refer to Rome in quite as obvious a manner as Lindsey would have us believe. In fact, Rome is not meant at all; Scripture is simply telling us about a whoring city that elevates itself above all other cities.[5]

---

4. See Cornelis Vanderwaal, *Openbaring van Jezus Christus* (Groningen, 1971), pp. 62ff.

5. See Vanderwaal, pp. 63-4.

We don't agree with Lindsey that the vision of the woman on the scarlet beast has to do with an event that will occur in the future. After all, the scarlet beast is none other than the beast in Revelation 13, which represented the godless state power that wars against the Church throughout the New Testament dispensation. The scarlet beast, too, is in league with satan, because it comes up out of "the bottomless pit" (17:8), which is satan's domain (see Rev. 9:11; 20:1,3). This tells us that to this beast, too, the dragon "gave his power and his throne and great authority" (13:2).

"The beast that you saw was, and is not, and is to ascend from the bottomless pit and go to perdition" (17:8 RSV). This beast existed in the past, sometimes disappears in the present, but reappears again.[6] Since no mention is made of 42 months, we are free to see this beast as being operative during both the Old and New Testament dispensations. In our New Testament time we see it at work: taken on a global scale, governments are heathen and satanic. A Christian government is a rarity. State power is beastly, except when the beast disappears for a while, such as when Constantine ruled. But it always reappears from out of the bottomless pit, until it goes to perdition (vs. 8,11).

---

6. B. Holwerda takes the statement that the beast "was, and is not" to mean that the beast existed earlier in successive world empires but that it collapsed and died when the Roman empire fell. The godless world power never revived after the Roman empire. "Therefore John was able to say, 'The beast doesn't exist today . . . .'" (p. 178).

The only problem with this explanation is that it concentrates too much on the situation of the church today, whereas the book of Revelation should first of all be seen in the context of its own time. Then we would see, as Holwerda admits, that the beast did exist in John's time, in the form of the Roman power.

We shouldn't try to identify the kings mentioned in verse 10; instead we should let the total image of the beast work its effect on us, so we will clearly see the main outlines: the heaps of sin on top of one another, the seven heads representing consecutive, yet in some sense unified, state powers, and the sentence of destruction. Whatever form the godless state power takes on, however long it may continue to influence history, its sure destiny is destruction. The image that John was shown was a traditional image; it is here used to indicate that God's judgment comes down on the godless state power. Let's not be guilty of using this vision to make our calculations about the end times.

We reject Lindsey's notion of a mystery religion of Babylon, as well as his attempt to identify the five kings mentioned in the vision of the woman on the scarlet beast. There is no talk at all here of an (apostate) religion that spreads its beliefs everywhere by cozying up to the political world power. Instead, we should see the woman riding on the dragon as symbolic of the apostate church trying to grab the power reins of world politics to further its own ends. That doesn't happen at some special time in the future but has always gone on in the history of the church. It is of the utmost importance to realize that we, right now, are living in the new era between Christ's ascension and His return. Throughout that era we find examples of the fulfillment of the prophecy about the woman.

In John's day, already, the Jews tried to mobilize Roman power against the church of Christ (Acts 13:50; 18:12; 21:27). Revelation talks about "the synagogue of Satan": Jews, who are not really such, in league with the Roman authorities against the church (2:9-10; 3:9). In the time of the Reformation, the unfaithful Roman Catholic Church used state power in its attempt to eradicate the new Protestant faith. Today we see the mammoth World Council of Churches trying to increase its influence in world politics, especially in the United Nations. The world religion grows as the Council lends its support to violence and plays into the hand of world Communism. Lindsey correctly points out the dangers of the Marxist-Christian dialogue that is so popular within that organization.

But as far as Lindsey's views about the end times are concerned, we must part ways with him. These views are too speculative, too much directed toward the future only, when in fact the apostate church has always made use of godless state power to wipe out the faithful church. It's true that this process is rising to a climax, as the rapid gains of the one world religion show. But we shouldn't use Revelation 17 to speculate about the end times.

14

Caught Up to Meet the Lord

"The Ultimate Trip"

In the chapter with the above-named title, Lindsey discusses the "Rapture," the sudden disappearance of millions of true believers to be with the Lord. They will vanish just like that while driving their cars, while playing championship football, and while attending college lectures. Not all will be taken, not even all those found regularly within the walls of the church. Their disappearance will be a great mystery to those who are left.

According to Lindsey, the Rapture is God's way of removing the faithful before the onslaught of the Antichrist and the False Prophet during the seven years of the Tribulation. He distinguishes the Rapture from Christ's return, which he calls Christ's second coming. Lindsey bases these ideas on two passages of Scripture, the first being the following:

I tell you this, brethren: flesh and blood cannot inherit the kingdom of God, nor does the perishable inherit the imperishable. Lo! I tell you a mystery. We shall not all sleep, but we shall all be changed, in a moment, in the twinkling of an eye, at the last trumpet. For the trumpet will sound, and the dead will be raised imperishable, and we shall be changed. For this perishable nature must put on the imperishable, and this mortal nature must put on immortality (I Cor. 15:50-3).

The second passage is I Thessalonians 4:13-18, according to which Jesus will descend from heaven and the believers will be caught up to meet Him in the air.

Both of these passages certainly describe the same event, but the question is: Which event? The onus is on Lindsey to prove that Scripture distinguishes between the Rapture and the return of Christ, and that these two passages in fact deal with the Rapture. Let's look at what he says.

I Corinthians 15:50-53

The crux of Lindsey's argument here is the word *mystery* in the sentence "Lo! I tell you a mystery."

The word "mystery" in the original Greek means something which has not been revealed before, but is now being revealed to those who are initiated. It was from this word that the concept of Greek fraternities came—everyone who has been in a fraternity or sorority knows there are certain secrets which are not disclosed until after initiation (PE, 128).

Everyone who believes in Christ as Savior is an initiate in the brotherhood of Christ. Lindsey says that whereas

only the initiates will be privy to the Rapture, the whole
world will see Christ's second return (Rev. 1:7).
"However, in the Rapture, only the Christians see
Him—it's a mystery, a secret. When the living believers
are taken out, the world is going to be mystified" (PE,
131). By this method of reasoning, Lindsey arrives at two
separate events: one which is secretive and mysterious,
and another which is public.

The problem with Lindsey's argument is that Paul
says something completely different when he uses the
word *mystery*. For Paul a mystery is always something in
God's redemptive plan that has been hidden but which,
in the New Testament dispensation, is being revealed to
all (see Rom. 16:25-6; Eph. 3:3ff). When Paul says "I tell
you a mystery," he is disclosing God's plan, and it no
longer remains a mystery or secret. This fact pulls the rug
from under Lindsey's argument and allows us to interpret
the passage as a discussion of the resurrection to take
place at Christ's return.

I Thessalonians 4:13-18

From I Thessalonians 4:13-18, Lindsey learns that
those who have fallen asleep in Jesus, meaning the
Christians who have died, will join the Lord first (PE,
130). But this is an incorrect reading of Paul, who says
that the believers who have died will be raised up first,
not that they will join the Lord first. In other words, their
resurrection will be the first point on Christ's agenda.
Next, according to Paul, we who are alive, who are left
(the Christians who are living at that time), will be
caught up together with them (the resurrected believers)
to meet the Lord in the air (vs. 16-17). Both groups will
meet the Lord simultaneously.

Why is Lindsey so sure that Paul is not talking about Christ's return?

> At the Rapture all the living believers will be caught up to join Him in the clouds.
> Here is the chief reason why we believe the Rapture occurs before the Tribulation: the prophets have said that God will set up a Kingdom on earth over which the Messiah will rule. There will be mortal people in that Kingdom. If the Rapture took place at the same time as the second coming, there would be no mortals left who would be believers; therefore, there would be no one to go into the Kingdom and repopulate the earth (PE, 132).

In our opinion, Lindsey's preconceptions lead him to believe that the meeting of Christ on the clouds by the believers and their reigning with Him in His Kingdom on earth are mutually exclusive. He would see things a little differently if he realized that the main point of this passage is Christ's descent from heaven to earth in all His glory, and that the believers' meeting Him is almost incidental.

Scripture calls our attention to the glorious and majestic character of Christ's return. He will be preceded by the voice of His herald, the archangel (possibly Michael). His cry of command signals the dead to rise so that they can hail Him as befits a king. The sound of the trumpet of God will accompany His descent, similar to the trumpets sounding when the emperor entered Rome. Trumpets are frequently mentioned in the book of Revelation; this trumpet is the last trumpet, the trumpet of God that accompanies the majestic return of Christ.[1]

---

1. Lindsey contradicts himself. He finds the Rapture predicted in I Thessalonians 4 and I Corinthians 15, passages in which we read about

(This reminds us of Exodus 19:16ff, where God descends on Mount Sinai to the sound of loud trumpets broadcasting His glory.)

The dead will rise. (In both I Thessalonians 4 and I Corinthians 15, Paul is speaking of one and the same resurrection. According to John 5:28-9, those who have done good deeds will be raised to the resurrection of life, and those who have done evil to the resurrection of judgment. In I Thessalonians 4 Paul is only talking about the believers.) Then both the dead in Christ who have been raised and the Christians still alive will be caught up to meet the Lord. Paul was concerned with reassuring the troubled believers in Thessalonica that those who had died would not miss out on Christ's glorious return. No, says Paul, we will all meet Him together, on the clouds. It will be the ascension of the Church. (This finds its parallel in Ex. 19:17: "Then Moses brought the people out of the camp to meet God.")

We will meet our Lord on the clouds, not so that we will be taken up into heaven, as Lindsey would have it, but so that we can give Him an appropriate welcome. Just as the Roman citizens went outside their city to hail the entering emperor, so we will rise to hail the descending King. There on the clouds we will share in Christ's display of majesty and power.[2] (In other passages of

---

the trumpet of God and the last trumpet sounding. "It seems difficult to reconcile this with the fact that the believers will be taken up before the events of Revelation 6-19. It is only with these events that trumpets begin to sound. When we read that we shall all be changed at the last trumpet, this must allude to the visible return of Christ to earth; this passage cannot be talking about the Rapture" (A. Berger and B. Vreugdenhil in *d'Econozel*, published by the "Vereniging van Gereformeerde Studenten," Rotterdam, March 1976, p. 50).

2. Remarks by Herman N. Ridderbos are of interest here, in *Paul:*

Scripture, clouds function as a symbol of God's majesty: see Psalm 97:2; Isaiah 19:1; Exodus 19:9,16). Then Christ will continue His triumphant descent to the earth, which will have been cleansed by fire. After that we will always be with Him and reign with Him in His eternal Kingdom of peace.[3]

We agree with Ridderbos when he observes that the Biblical description of the events surrounding Christ's return is fragmentary and inadequate for developing a complete and systematic picture of these events (*Paul*, p. 554). However, a certain order of events is visible. First the believers who have died will be resurrected; with the living believers they will meet Christ on the clouds in glory. Then the unbelievers will be raised up (Rev. 20:12-13; Dan. 12:2).

The believers will participate in their judgment (Rev. 20:11ff; I Cor. 6:2). Next, death, as the last enemy, will be destroyed (Rev. 20:14; I Cor. 15:26). Finally the New Jerusalem will descend from heaven (Rev. 21:2ff), where the believers will reign forever (Rev. 22:5).

We conclude that Lindsey is wrong in finding a suggestion of the Rapture in I Thessalonians 4:13-18, or anywhere else in Scripture. The idea of a Rapture is

---

An Outline of his Theology (Eerdmans, 1975), pp. 531-7. See especially p. 536, which deals with our rising to hail Christ.

3. Other phrasings in Scripture elucidate the meaning of "we shall always be with the Lord" (I Thess. 4:17). II Timothy 2:12 says that "we shall . . . reign with Him." In Romans 5:17 we read on the one hand that "death reigned," but on the other hand that through grace and righteousness, the believers "reign in life through the one man Jesus Christ." According to Romans 8:17, "to be with him" is to be "glorified with him" and to be "fellow heirs with Christ." It means we have an "inheritance in the kingdom of Christ" (Eph. 5:5). See Ridderbos, *Paul*, p. 562.

IMPORTANT

foreign to the Scriptures. The passages that we have looked at describe the one and only coming of Christ which we are to expect. We can apply Lindsey's words "There's nothing that remains to be fulfilled before Christ could catch [you] up to be with Him" (PE, 134) to that coming of Christ. With an eye to His coming, Paul says, "The day of the Lord will come like a thief in the night. But you are not in darkness, brethren, for that day to surprise you like a thief" (I Thess. 5:2,4).

Watch therefore! Christ may return any day!